COLLECTING DRAWINGS

COLLECTING DRAWINGS

by

KEN ETHERIDGE

LONDON
G. BELL AND SONS

FIRST PUBLISHED 1970

PUBLISHED BY G. BELL & SONS LTD.
YORK HOUSE PORTUGAL STREET LONDON WC2

ISBN 0 7135 1579 1

PRINTED IN GREAT BRITAIN BY
WILLIAM CLOWES AND SONS, LIMITED
LONDON AND BECCLES

Contents

The Illustrations

7

The drawing by Edward Calvert on the title page is reproduced by permission of the Trustees of the British Museum.

Glossary of Terms

'AFTER': a drawing in the style of another artist.

BISTRE: a brownish ink or wash made from wood or peat ash.

BODY-COLOUR: gouache or poster-paint or watercolour thickened by adding Chinese white.

CAPRICCIO: a fanciful composition, based on landscape, sculpture or architectural motifs.

GRANULATION: grains of colour sinking into the crevices in the paper to give a mottled effect.

GRISAILLE: the modelling of figures, landscape or architectural details, carried out in grey, brown or terre verte. This is usually a preliminary stage, though some drawings may be completed in this technique.

'HEIGHTENED WITH WHITE': a drawing on tinted paper with the highlights touched with Chinese white or any other solid body-colour; white or any other chalk of a light colour may be used in the same way on grey or tinted paper to bring out the highlights.

IMPASTO: thick paint, modelled to suggest the form of objects or texture of surfaces.

LUGT: Collector's marks, with details of the drawing's provenance, history and any other relevant literature. Fritz Lugt was an art historian who collected the marks and heraldic devices, seen on drawings; he also included a reference book listing.

'LAID DOWN': the drawing has been pasted or glued on to a thick card, mount or board.

MAT: the mount. 'Matted': mounted. (American terms[1].)

'RECTO': the right side or face of a drawing.

SEPIA: a dark brown ink or paint, or watercolour washes of this tint.

SOOT-WATER: an ink or paint made from soot and water with the addition of gum, honey, barley-sugar or any other adhesive.

'SCHOOL':   the period or style of a drawing: e.g. 'English school' or 'Dutch School'.

'STUDY':   a rough sketch or preliminary drawing.

'SQUARED FOR TRANSFER':   a drawing with ruled lines, usually squares: a device used for transferring the drawing onto another paper or canvas of a larger size.

'SURROUND':   the mount or board round a drawing, or the space between the drawing and the mount. (The 'mat' in American terminology[1].)

TERRE VERTE: a greyish green paint.

'VERSO':   the back or underside of a drawing, which may also have a study or sketch.

---

[1] These terms are used in the book *Watercolour: Materials and Technique* by George Dibble, University of Utah.   (Holt, Rinehart and Winston, Inc.)

1. Introduction

THE term 'drawing' in the trade and in the salerooms denotes a work in pencil, charcoal, pen and ink or crayon of any colour, executed usually on paper, and by extension of the meaning one tinted with watercolour and finally a watercolour painting itself. In modern parlance a 'drawing' is therefore any work in watercolour, whether it contains any drawing in the strict sense of linear work with the pen or pencil or is simply a direct painting in watercolour.

Up until about 1805, when the practice of drawing the landscape carefully in pen and ink began to go out of fashion among artists, the watercolours were what the name implied: stained drawings with colour only added as a decorative element to an otherwise perfectly satisfactory work of art. The calligraphy was of a high order. A number of the artists were, in fact, engravers, or prepared drawings for engravers to whom they were apprenticed, and a carefully designed composition, finished in every detail, was expected of them. Local colour—that is the actual colour of objects in the landscape such as trees, buildings, rocks and figures—was then added over the shading, which was made in grey, sepia or black in conjunction with the ink outlines, the tones being carefully graded to suggest recession and perspective.

Artists such as Dayes, Varley, and even Turner and Girtin in their apprentice days, followed this method. 'Topographical' artists they are sometimes called with just a note of contempt, because they drew all the details of the landscape to satisfy the public demand. They were the cameras of the age. and their rapportage gave a very welcome service to those who could not travel, but loved to see the wonders of foreign countries and also

the more inaccessible places of beauty in Britain. It was the age
of the traveller—the traveller in Britain as well as the wealthy
young man who could afford to do the 'Grand Tour'.

A competent artist almost always accompanied the traveller
who then wrote his book and had engravings made to illustrate
it. These may have been done by the artist himself or by a
professional engraver, using his sketches. I have one such
engraving of Tintern Abbey, and in the left-hand corner is the
phase 'Dep. T. Girton', a minor artist not to be confused with
Girtin. Girton had made a drawing on the spot, which was then
used to make an engraving by Alken and included in a book
'A Walk Through Wales in August 1797 by the Rev. Richard
Warner. The book I saw was in its third edition, obviously
selling well.

The engraver imposed certain demands upon the artist: accuracy
of line and careful attention to composition as well as the produc-
tion of a 'finished' drawing with all the variations of line and
texture and tone that the engraver could use to display his
virtuosity and enrich his design. Trees had to be drawn in detail;
rivers and lakes suggested with carefully drawn reflections;
architectural motifs had to be in correct perspective and with the
attention to detail then in fashion. Figures were always drawn
to make the scene more interesting and to add scale to the composition. The pointing figure in the foreground became almost
a pictorial cliché; the local characters at work—fishermen,
washerwomen, haymakers, etc., added a touch of human interest;
pictures began to 'tell a story', no doubt with the influence of
Claude and Poussin and Rosa already seeping into English landscape art. The classical method of composition was almost
always used with foreground, middle distance and distance. (See
sketch Chap. 3.)

Whether the discipline of the engraver was a good or a bad
thing is a moot point that I have not the scope here to discuss;
topographical accuracy was the desired result; but such accuracy
among the commercial artists of the times—and they were little
more than this—had a stultifying effect on the drawing. Too
often they were content with a set performance: a certain tech-

nique of loops or running curves for foliage; a pattern of lines for architecture; a classical arrangement of foreground, middle distance and distance for all the compositions; the shadowed foreground and carefully placed 'ruin'. It required the genius of a Rowlandson or a Varley (and some of their works are also a little arid and tired in technique!) to produce pictures of charm and distinction. Their colour washes, which were introduced into the engravings too, gave the first indication that the artist in watercolour was trying his wings. Young Girtin and Cotman finally found the way to fly, but more of that later.

Collecting 'drawings' is, then, a rather specialized hobby. It needs taste—and this can be developed—and discrimination in the choice of artists. It needs, too, a certain flair for recognizing forgotten or neglected artists and for rescuing some unknown from oblivion. Collectors of china can tell by the 'feel' of a cup or a dish whether it is the one they are seeking: collectors of drawings after a while also develop a sixth sense; the colours and tones of a period will be recognized; the tricks of technique of certain artists, the subjects they liked. The experienced collector will 'know' that the drawing is by Cotman or Girtin or Crome, whatever the catalogue says. He has an instinct for the genuine and a shying away from the doubtful; and he will not be afraid to back his judgment in the saleroom or the antique shop.

That is where the excitement comes in: rummaging through a parcel at Sotheby's or Christie's and seeing an item that is outstanding amongst the mediocre stuff, then bidding for it and getting it at a reasonable price. This happened to me recently. A parcel of drawings in 'folio' (contained between a large folded sheet of white paper) was offered for sale at Sotheby's. There were six little drawings in all. One I recognized as a drawing in pen and ink by Sir Joshua Reynolds, lightly touched with watercolours. On closer examination I found the signature of Sir Joshua at the bottom of the drawing and the name of the sitter 'LADY ANNE PAGE—(PAGET?)' in the artist's flamboyant scrawl. The costume and the style were correct. I fell in love with it and decided to try to buy it for my collection. I bid up to £12 and found only one other bidder against me. The bidding went up

to £14 and I finally got it for £16. The remainder of the parcel
consisted of drawings by Edridge, and William Joy; so I was
quite pleased with my bargain. My Reynolds drawing now
hangs in my study, framed and mounted and all the more valued
because I picked it up in such a way (Plate 4).

One is not always so lucky, of course. A drawing which I
bought afterwards in a junk shop in the fond hope that it was a
Girtin was identified by the British Museum as one by James
Bourne, a prolific artist who toured the west and seems to have
absorbed the 'influences' of his times to good effect.

That is the fascination and the pitfall of collecting drawings.
The greats stand out clearly, and the second-rate ones follow in a
multitude: there are over 350 listed in Martin Hardie's index of
the eighteenth century alone![1] Sometimes they catch an echo
of the glory and imitate the masters so cleverly that it is difficult
to tell them apart at a glance. Collectors also have the weakness
of seeing all their geese as swans, or fondly hoping that the ugly
duckling may turn out to be one. But it must not be forgotten
that the great ones were once beginners and copyists of their
masters.

Young Thomas Girtin imitated Dayes, and he and Turner
copied engravings of the great paintings of the time in the house
of Dr. Monro; and what young artist of talent will be content with
just copying? He will soon be adding his own touches and his
own peculiar vision of the world and confusing future collectors
with the puzzle. Is the drawing a Girtin, or a copy by Girtin
of a work by Dayes, or a drawing in the style of Dayes? Echoes
will persist in the lesser artist: the more talented will absorb them
even more deeply with his finer sensibilities; imitation follows
admiration to such an extent that the gifted young draughtsman
will give a very close rendering of his model's style.

Artists have always been prone to imitate their betters to make
a sale (by no means a trait confined to the eighteenth century!)
and it is often very difficult to make a decision. Critics are only
human, and collectors are blinded by affection to see swans in

[1] *Water-Colour Painting in Britain*, Vol. 1, 1967.

every goose-herd; but on the other hand they may pass over a cygnet who looks very much the ugly duckling when young.

Let us not forget that all the great artists were once young, too, learning their craft, trying their hands; the apprentices did not produce masterpieces all at once; even Michelangelo tried his hand on a stone cupid, imitating the antique. And to good effect, too. He sold it to one of the wealthy collectors of his day! We must not pass over a drawing 'attributed' to Cotman or Constable because it is not up to his usual brilliance. It may well be an early work. Or done on an 'off' day. The glimpse of genius in Turner's *Liber Studiorum* drawings are, for me, just as fascinating as his full-scale orchestration of colour and light: in fact, more so; they show the giant spirit struggling to release itself from the chains of convention. The artist is Prometheus, chained to the rock. We are aware almost too painfully of the chains, but he is still Prometheus, who stole fire from the gods.

It behoves the ambitious collector, then, to know something of his subject. I shall give in the next few chapters a description of some of the artists most representative of their times, but first a description of the techniques involved. The collector will then, I hope, be able to choose his drawings with some knowledge and certainty.

2. Technique and Materials

NO one can fully appreciate drawing and watercolour painting without having some insight into the technical difficulties of this fragile medium; indeed, a little practice will give one a greater respect and admiration for the triumphs of the masters. And I trust that this book will fall into the hands of the true collector—one who likes to gather round him the best examples of the art because he loves them for what they are—an enrichment of heart and mind by association with the tenderest and most gentle spirits of the past. For watercolour is indeed a gentle art, almost feminine in its delicacy, but capable in the hands of the giants of expressing a depth and largeness of vision, which belie the implied femininity: it is a remarkable thing that there are so few women artists who excel in watercolour; one can recall only Angelica Kauffmann and Eloise Stannard, neither of them in the first rank. Among the moderns, Helen Alingham and Gwen John produced many good drawings, though the latter's crayon and pencil drawings cannot be classed as true watercolours. Perhaps the medium requires a degree of perspicacity and tenaciousness that only men can give. The weak go to the wall and the strong soar, grappling with the difficulties and fashioning swords out of the sorrows.

The first question we have to answer is: what is a watercolour? Does it mean a work in full colour? Or may we include pencil and crayon drawings, and tinted pen and ink sketches? Iolo Williams in his invaluable book *Early English Watercolours* writes: 'Normally, when people speak of a watercolour, they mean one in full colour, one in which the subject is represented in something approaching its natural range and variety of hue. But it must be remembered that there are also many watercolours in monochrome washes—whether Indian ink, sepia, bistre, blue, grey or what not—and especially in landscape topography, it would be absurd to exclude them from a book on English watercolour.'

These monochrome drawings were the beginnings of water-colour painting in Britain. The ink, used with a quill or reed pen, could be black, brown, grey, or even red, as in some of Turner's sketches.[1] The ink drawing could be made over a lightly pencilled outline, or the ink could be added later to 'strengthen' the forms: Inigo Jones did this over drawings, exe-cuted with sepia washes, to bring out details of costume and architecture; it is obvious, too, that Turner used a pen to describe some of the buildings, when these almost disappeared in his luminous mists. Diluted ink could be used effectively to suggest distance: Rowlandson, Devis, Varley and Dayes employ this method. Strong, undiluted ink is used in the foreground; a lighter tone of the same colour suggests the middle distance; a very pale tint of diluted ink is used in the background. The washes repeat this formula. In this way the drawing is given depth and perspective. A brush (or 'pencil' as it was then called) could be used, too, as Gainsborough does in some of his landscapes, suggesting the feathery masses of the foliage with a light sweep of the brush (Plate 11).

Drawing with a reed pen or a quill was a very necessary accomplishment for the topographical artist. The nice point as to whether such drawings are works of art is tentatively answered by Iolo Williams: 'Topography has been defined as the portraiture of places. The topographer's job is to produce a drawing which will be recognized as representing a certain place—whether it be a group of mountains, a stretch of pastoral country, a street in a town, a gentleman's country seat—and will record its features for posterity. Landscape is the imaginative manipulation of natural features such as hills, trees, rivers, fields, clouds and so forth into a composition which will be aesthetically pleasing or

[1] The appreciation of 'line' in drawing is discussed in detail in *Drawing* by Daniel M. Mendelowitz, Holt, Rinehart & Winston, 1967. He particularizes the mechanical, contour, spontaneous, virtuoso, fragmented, calligraphic, lyric and flowing line.

2

otherwise impressive.' The author points out that the two categories overlap considerably, and that the more skilful of the topographical artists always modify their subjects or rearrange them slightly in an attempt to appear 'picturesque' or impressive. So it is not possible to dub one artist 'topographical' and dismiss him as a kind of human camera without trying to ascertain whether he has indeed only made a 'copy' of the scene before him. A good deal of art comes into it, if only in the manipulation of the pen and ink.

The early artist had to make his own ink and carry it with him. Alexander Cozens travelled to Italy in 1740, taking lamp black and gum for making ink. A rough and ready substitute was soot, or burnt-wood resin or peat (called 'bistre', a warmer, brownish tint). Honey, barley-sugar or gum-arabic formed the binding medium, when mixed with water.

These binding materials were also used with the colours which early artists obtained from natural sources: what we still call the 'earth' colours are self-explanatory. Ochre, raw sienna and the kindred light reds and burnt siennas were from the soil. They were washed and mixed by the artist and stored in shells or little saucers for use.

Then in 1776 came the first dealer of ready-made colours, advertised by Matthew Danby as 'transparent colours for stained drawings', and was followed by the firm of Reeves in 1780. They made up the colours into little cakes. Other firms imitated these and manufactured as well little saucers for mixing the colours.

Dayes had kept his colours in moulds of card. Winsor and Newton soon supplied them in pans, kept moist by the addition of honey or glycerine. Arranging the pans in little boxes for transport was the next step, and so evolved the paintbox. Tubes followed about 1848, but the colours in tubes had to be kept moister to facilitate the squeezing out and more glycerine had to be added. This is still the case, and some artists prefer the cakes on the ground that they are more pure and dry more quickly. Glycerine may still be used to slow up the drying process; on the other hand some form of alcohol accelerates this: Paul Sandby used gin! This may have been the reason, too, why James Roberts suggested that 'Porter is a very good general wash'[1] Waiting for a large, general wash to dry can be very tedious, if one is busy.

The paper on which the artist laid his ink and colours varied a good deal; seldom was it pure white in the eighteenth century or earlier. Oatmeal, cream, grey were the usual tints, and the imperfections of the paper often resulted in stains and spots on the surface. David Cox made these 'fly away' by changing them into little birds. John Varley sometimes painted on grey paper which he laid on a white card and obtained the high-lights by scraping out with a knife, so that the white card was revealed. Some papers were very thin.[2]

Tinting the paper with washes of colour, tea, coffee, porter or beer, gave it an interesting 'glow' so much admired in emulation of the golden tone of the landscapes of Claude and Poussin. Watercolour, being a transparent medium, showed this ground in all parts of the painting. Chinese white as a ground gave paintings an enamelled effect in Hunt's and Melville's work.[3]

Dayes and Cotman, in their topographical drawings, made elaborate ink outlines of every detail before embarking on colour. The ink outline was in itself a work of art. I have a signed Cotman drawing of trees on a river bank, which is infinitely graceful and tender. The fact that the drawing is signed implies, I think, that the artist regarded it as a finished work. The ink outline was *de rigueur* until about 1819, when James Roberts advises the student not to use pen and ink because the pen 'destroys softness, breadth and atmosphere and gives the drawing the stiff and formal effect of bad-coloured engraving.'[4] He suggested

[1] *Introductory Lessons for Painting in Watercolours*, 1819.

[2] John Downman observed a pink stain at the back of one of his drawings, daubed by a naughty offspring, and liked the effect of this so much that he used the method to suggest the colour of cheeks in his portraits, painting this colour on the *back* of the paper!

[3] Linen or silk was also used. Crawhall's animal drawings were made in this way. He probably sized the fabrics first, then flooded on his colour with directness and economy of line and form.

[4] *Introductory Lessons for Painting in Watercolours*, 1819.

~instead a pencil outline and washes of diluted colour made from red ink, gamboge, raw sienna, ochre or 'tobacco steeped in water'.[1]

After making an ink outline, the artist of the eighteenth century then suggested the modelling with washes of grey, sepia or bistre: hills, trees, buildings and figures were shaded in this way by the application of graded washes, sometimes fading into the white paper by softening the edges with a damp brush, sometimes with darker washes dropped in or superimposed. The local colour, such as the green of the trees or the red and blues of buildings or costumes, was then added as a last coat.

Body-colour or opaque colour was sometimes added for the high-lights. Van Dyck used opaque colour (another name for it is 'gouache'), so did Inigo Jones.[2] Distemper was used by Richard Wilson with similar effect. Many artists combined all methods with happy results: Robertson employed ink outlines and transparent washes in his distant landscapes and made the trees in the foreground more richly solid by touching them up with body-colour. Calcott and Havell have landscapes painted almost entirely in body-colour; so have Turner and Birket Foster. The solid colour extends the range and gives the painting an 'oilish' quality, but the purists are not happy about it and maintain that this is trespassing on the domains of oil-painting and not really true watercolour technique at all.

Another attempt at emulating the richness and depth of oils was the varnishing of watercolours. John Varley's later paintings have this method. William Hamilton does this, too. I have a painting of his of a girl at a cottage door, which is varnished, giving the darker tones a velvety quality, not unattractive, although an unpleasant, uneven shine appears in some parts of the painting (Plate 3).

Only with the advent of Girtin and Cotman were the local colours and shadows of the landscape painted directly, that is,

---

[1] *Introductory Lessons for Painting in Watercolours,* 1819.

[2] In miniature painting a thin coat of starch and gum or sugar was first laid on as a ground. *The Gentleman's Exercise* (1607) by Henry Peacham, recommends this as the best way to start painting 'limnings' (miniatures).

without a preliminary undercoat. Shadows were made luminous, skies and clouds and figures given more richness of colour, the 'direct' method using the reflecting qualities of the paper to give full luminosity to the paint. Even the darkest tones—see the watercolours of Peter de Wint and Russell Flint—if painted directly, can have a glowing intensity.

There is a danger in the super-imposing of many washes: a muddiness may result, especially as the colours of the early artists were not at all pure, and the addition of honey or gum arabic of a very crude quality did not help.

I have not mentioned the use of crayon. This could be used as a shading medium as well as ink. Gainsborough drew with charcoal, combining this with solid white in the highlights. This method of modelling was similar to the 'grisaille' of the old masters, who modelled their figures in grey or terre verte and superimposed glazes to suggest the local colours. The watercolour artists no doubt realized that this method could lend itself very easily to the transparent washes of watercolour.

A word must be said here about the medium.

'Every medium has, so to speak, its own tempo. The tempo of a pencil or piece of charcoal is quite different from the tempo of a woodcut. But the habit of mind which creates, for instance, a pen drawing cannot simply be applied mechanically to the making of a woodcut; to do this would be to deny the validity of the spiritual as well as the technical tempo.' One may add to Karl Knappe's dictum, that the tempo or speed of working in a watercolour is also different from that of a drawing. The artist with a brush in his hand explores the possibilities of quickly-applied washes, watches them drying, regulates his second or third addition of colour according to the state of the first wash. Happy or gauche serendipity comes into it. Girtin and Cotman could time the second dropping in of colour to perfection. Shotter-Boys had to wait until the first wash was completely dry before he could use the 'dragged brush" technique; so had Girtin, when applying the broken washes and blobs of colour; a damp first wash would have spoilt the effect. So to speak of 'tempo' is not altogether a fanciful term; it is a reality of technique.

Watercolour, like every other medium, has its own 'language', its own idiom of expression, which gives effects that cannot be expressed in any other medium.

It is this special language that watercolourists learn and respect; we have seen how some artists try to make their pictures look like oil-paintings by the use of gouache or varnishing. The stretching of the possibilities of the medium in this way may lead to new horizons—or to disaster.

Washes could, of course, be manipulated in many ways: Francis Nicholson used his famous 'stopping out' process. He used a mixture of beeswax, turpentine and flake white, which he painted over those parts of the drawing where the high-lights appeared. He would then proceed with the painting in the usual way and lift off the 'stopping-out' medium with turpentine or spirits of wine at the end, revealing the white paper. Girtin discovered a similar process by accidentally dropping water on to his painting; when lifted off with a clean rag, he noticed that the paint lifted too. He used this method sometimes to suggest high-lights on rocks and foliage. David Cox often used a fine blade to scrape out ripples on water or high-lights on foliage. Turner used another method—sandpaper—rubbed over a dry wash to scrape away some of the paint and reveal the white paper. A sponge or rag, even his fingers or the wooden end of the brush, were sometimes employed, too, for this effect. Washing out was also used by De Wint and Cox and many others. After scraping out or sandpapering or washing out, the resultant pale areas could, of course, be washed over with another colour: some of Turner's skies achieve their scintillating effect in this way; pale pinks or yellows appear mixed in little flecks with the darker blues or greys, anticipating the flickering, prismatic hues of the French Impressionists.

The manipulation of the brush is, of course, an important element in all painting techniques. Cotman could apply a second wash with a full brush and leave parts of the first wash showing to suggest texture. David Cox could use short, criss-cross or diagonal strokes of the brush in the second wash to modify the colour of the first and suggest movement of clouds or grass-blades in the wind. Girtin and De Wint could drop in large blobs of colour when the first wash was almost dry. I have already mentioned the 'dragged brush' technique of Shotter-Boys; a dry or full brush would add variations to this method. Turner, Cotman and Bonington may be examined carefully for their subtle use of all these methods. John Varley, too, although of the old school, knew most of the tricks and could use them with telling effect.

Small spots or stippling with the brush was a technique frequently employed to give the texture of foliage (Crome) or the fur of animals (Hills and Howitt), herbage and masonry (Varley, Prout) or the richness and patina of costumes and still life. W. H. Hunt perfected this method for his meticulous renderings of fruit, flowers and nests. Rossetti and Burne-Jones scrubbed, stippled and overpainted for rich textures.

Brushes varied in size as they do now; Samuel Palmer had a two-inch wide sable, which he used, filled with colour ready mixed in pans. The peculiar, clotted look of some of his colours may be attributed to this manner of working: the glycerine in the composition of the colours had probably collected in the bottom of the pans and he used this in his very full and wet washes; he used pen and ink, gouache and transparent glazes too. Birket Foster obviously used a very small sable. The minute touches of gouache he liked so much to suggest foliage, grass-blades and cloud, as well as the delicate features of his figures could only have been done in this way. John Glover invented a split brush, so that the sections of the brush could more easily depict foliage. The small, stippled dots were used by the Pre-Raphaelites, too. Rossetti was fond of superimposing a tint of blue in gouache on a first wash of another blue, giving a deep, glowing and scintillating colour; gold, rose-pink and vermilion he applied in the same way.

Yet another method of varying the surface texture was invented by John Sell Cotman, and followed by his son, John Joseph—that of mixing sour paste with his colours. This had the effect of slowing up the drying and giving the artist the chance to manipulate the wash still further by the addition of other tints; and the thickening of the paint gave an opportunity to suggest the form of leaves and rocks in the strokes of the brush. This is rather akin to the technique of impasto painting in oils. A painting, using this method, is in my collection. *The Windmill in Marshland* by John Joseph Cotman is one of his gold and blue period. The pen and brown ink outline is visible in one corner and the paste has given a soft, misty effect to the distant town and the reflections in the water (Plate 13).

The wax crayon method is a modern innovation, and can be seen in the watercolours of Piper, Moore and Sutherland. The artist rubbed a wax crayon—white or pale yellow or pink—over some parts of the drawing, then proceeded to wash over the sketch with the second coat of colour. This refused to adhere to the areas treated with the wax crayon, leaving a mottled, broken colour, the tiny droplets suggesting rough stone or the coarse texture of cloth or flesh. Henry Moore's shelter sketches use this technique. Wax crayon and red or brown crayon combined with pencil or ink give a most original and telling effect that conveys the agony and the anxiety of the people in the shelters. Piper used the method in his landscapes, and the bombed houses and broken farms he depicts have the same desolate air; the richness of his technique, combining as he does pen and ink, gouache and watercolour washes put on directly in broad sweeps, makes a very personal and powerful statement. Sutherland in the same way in his *Bestiary* and in his landscape sketches achieves a semi-abstract rendering of the subject.

Modern handmade papers are admirable for these elaborate techniques, and it must be remembered that the artists of earlier times were unable to manipulate their papers in this way, because the surface would not stand a deal of scrubbing or overloading with colour, etc. Drawing paper in the seventeenth and eighteenth centuries was handmade and sized by the artist himself.[1] Sheets were quite small and when made into sketch-books they were hardly ever more than about ten inches across, which accounts for the fact that many artists like Towne and Cotman

[1] Miniatures or 'limnings' of the sixteenth century were painted on thin vellum, mounted on fine card. The favourite ground of the eighteenth century was ivory, first used by Richard Cosway.

sometimes painted across a double leaf of their sketch-books. (The crease is visible in the centre.) The papers were soft in tone, but too fragile to allow scraping or washing out.

When Whatman produced tougher handmade papers in the mid-eighteenth century, artists could experiment more, and some like Cox explored the possibilities of grey or oatmeal Scotch paper, which had a rough texture. Some of his most charming evocations of atmosphere and light are to be seen on this kind of paper.

A little knowledge of the materials will help the collector to realize how the artists achieved their effects; he will look for the different technique—the 'language' of each particular artist, which is as idiosyncratic as his hand in writing—and he will be able to recognize with experience the work of the artist.

As Turner once remarked, he mixes his paint 'with brains', but also by the light of an inner vision, which transforms the world. Like Michelangelo digging into 'the white meat of Carrara', as he called it, to release the form hidden there, the artist will delve into the mysteries of painting until he achieves the desired effect; the master with the economy of perfect technique, the less gifted by laborious and sometimes mistaken means: the viewer will guess which is which. The lesser lights, however, are not to be despised: the Prouts and Havells and Rowbothams have their charms, too. We are not always in the mood for the rare-fied heights of Cotman, Girtin and Turner. The more homely levels of Crome and Wimperis have a lasting value—they are sincere attempts at depicting nature, interpreting the scene; and all sincerity and true affection is to be valued as we value the conversation of a talented man.

Inspired drawings record the conversation of giants with the world they know; we shall read them again as long as men may look and enjoy the comments of bright souls.

Confronted by a landscape or figure, the artist realizes that he has to make a compromise; he cannot draw everything; and it is this struggle with reality, and the ultimate victory of the artist over the material world that fades visibly before his eyes, which makes his drawing a masterwork. I say 'drawing' advisedly.

It involves direct appraisal of the landscape or form and a sincere translation into another language of lines and tones on the page: the fusion of eye and hand and heart in that moment of truth that is caught forever, if he is a good artist, who explores as he looks.[1]

All drawing is revelation; the heart and mind is in the exploration of form; the affection is in its recording; style is the personality and the experience and the mastery of the various facets of technique and in the selection of facts and the means used to record them. The choice of colours, the arrangement of tone values, the nervous exploration of line, the welding of all these into an individual composition—these show us, not only the artist's background and education, but the time and place of his living; we see his friends in his influences; we see his hopes and ideals—(the ghost of Claude walks through Wilson, and Wilson whispers to Sandby[2] and the giant calm of Canaletto breathes over Girtin's panoramas); we see his struggles to express heroic vision, heaven and hell in the tortured figures of Blake, all the gods of the Parthenon awakening and stretching their limbs again in the Neo-classicists, lost Atlantis and the glories of Arthur's chivalry flickering a wan flame in the Pre-Raphaelites, and in the best of De Wint and Cotman and Constable, an abiding record of the love of the countryside which is every Briton's heritage.

[1] '(Drawings) achieve much of their distinction from the fact that they have been produced not for public consumption, but only to satisfy the painter's enquiring mind.' *Drawing* by Daniel M. Mendelowitz, Holt, Rinehart & Winston.

[2] I have a little sketch by Paul Sandby, called THE TEMPLE OF VENUS, based on a painting by Richard Wilson.

A brief History of Watercolour Painting

3. The Eighteenth Century

RTISTS of the continental schools used watercolour from the earliest times, combined with bistre, ink or pencil, either as preliminary sketches for larger oil paintings and portraits or as works in their own right. Albrecht Dürer (1471–1528) was among the first to give watercolour that distinctive drawing and affectionate observation of natural detail which we have now learned to expect in a well-made drawing. The artist took obvious delight in recording the details of the landscape, and also had a feeling for aerial perspective and the effects of light which point forward to the great efflorescence of the eighteenth and nineteenth century in Britain.

Lucas Cranach (1515–1586) and Hans Holbein the younger (1487–1545) made tinted portrait sketches, and in the Netherlands Paul Bril (1554–1626) and Tobias Verhaegt (1561–1631) with their brown and blue-washed landscapes achieved great subtlety of effect.[1] More variety of colour was introduced by Roeland Savery (1576–1639) Adriaen van Ostade (1610–1685) and Cornelius Duaert of the same period. Their drawings were sold as completed pictures and were rightly regarded as finished works of art.

Pen and ink and watercolour was a flexible and easily-transportable medium for recording the new discoveries of the Elizabethan era. John White, sailing with Sir Richard Grenville, made many such drawings in Virginia. Birds, plants, fish and human figures in native costume appear in his drawings. At home

---

[1] Early drawings by Turner use a similar technique.

Nicholas Hilliard and Isaac Oliver among the 'limners' produced miniatures of young noblemen and their families, which were close enough in technique to the illuminations of earlier times for some critics to see a continuous tradition in the art of watercolour painting.   But Puritanism put an end to any traditional movement in Britain, inspiration and guidance coming from the continent.   Some of the artists came too: Rubens and Van Dyck practised watercolour painting, and an inventory of the goods of Charles I shows a list of many 'water cullours'.

The Dutch artists, however, produced drawings only as a small proportion of their *œuvre*: the later watercolourists in England were specialists, delighting to explore all the possibilities of the medium, to widen and deepen its scope and achieve subtleties and richnessess of expression as never before.

This seems an appropriate place to describe the artists 'in small' who painted miniatures in Britain.   These little works of art can be considered as drawings, as most of them were executed in a watercolour medium.   The word 'miniature' was derived from the Latin verb *miniare*—to paint with minium, the red pigment used to decorate the initial letters of manuscripts.   We use the term 'miniature' today to describe any small work of art, but it originally meant the painted letters or decorations in illuminated scripts.

This may have been the origin of miniature portraits; or they may have begun as a small painting of the writer, appended to or near the signature on court documents.   Another theory is that they were based on the Renaissance fashion of wearing medallions which bore the portraits of friends or family, derived from Roman customs of the fourth and fifth centuries.   These medallions were circular; and this shape was that of the early sixteenth-century miniatures in the time of Henry VIII.   Oval and rectangular shapes were introduced at the end of the century.

Vellum was the foundation, stuck on to very fine card.   Colours were ground by the artist, mixed with a little powdered gumarabic and sugar.[1]   The mixture was then stored and hot water

---

[1] A contemporary reference to Shakespeare's 'sugared sonnets' testifies to the custom of adding sugar to ink to give it gloss.

added when required for painting. A coat of starch and gum
was first given to the vellum, as described by Henry Peacham in
The Gentleman's Exercise. He goes on to particularize the method
of working: 'according to the generall complexion of the face you
are to draw, lay on a weake colour, that done, trace out the eyes,
nose, mouth and eare, with lake or red Lead, and if the complexion
be swarthy, adde either of Sea coale, lampe blacke to deepen and
shadow it, when you have thus done, lay it by for a day, or till
it be well dry, then by little and little, worke it with a curious
hand with the liuely colour, till you have brought it to perfection.' The paintings show what they meant by 'perfection', and
it can clearly be seen that it is the pure method of watercolour
in transparent washes that is used. The ground could be varied
to suit the complexion of the sitters. (Some artists had a number
of pieces of vellum ready painted in varying shades of pink or
flesh-colour, and chose the one most suitable for the sitter.)
Backgrounds were usually blue in the sixteenth century, though
Hilliard and Cooper introduced charming landscape details into
many of their portraits.

Nicholas Hilliard (1547–1619) and Samuel Cooper (1609–1672)
were among the most prolific and famous limners. Hilliard liked
the three-quarters left view of the face, a style followed closely by
his son Nicholas (1581–1640). Cooper showed continental
influences and his landscape backgrounds were more elaborate and
sophisticated.

John Hoskins (d. 1665) made many copies of the paintings of
Van Dyck and their style influenced his own miniatures which are
bolder and freer in treatment. He used a greenish stippling in the
faces, which is characteristic of his work.

The stippling method was further elaborated by C. P. Crosse
(1630–1716?) who used a greenish blue, and his son Lawrence red
and blue in the flesh. Backgrounds varied, with swags of curtains
as well as landscapes.

The name of the sitter, the family crest or motto as well as the
initials of the artist were added with pure gold dust. This was
mixed with powdered gum and kept in shells until required, hence
the term 'shell gold'.

These artists were proficient in other media, too. Isaac Oliver produced many drawings in crayon and pen and ink, and also painted larger pictures with landscape backgrounds. He delighted in depicting the elaborate embroideries and jewellery of the period with consummate skill.

There were further technical developments in the seventeenth century. J. Toutin, a French goldsmith, applied thin colour washes to white enamel, which was then re-fired, retaining the true colour of the watercolour. 'Plumbago' miniatures also became fashionable (from the Latin 'plumbum'—graphite) the portrait being drawn in pure graphite on vellum or paper with stippling to shade the face and background.[1] Ivory as a base was perfected by Richard Cosway and remained a favourite, the white, untouched, or covered with a very thin wash, being used for high-lights.

Richard Cosway produced hundreds of miniatures of the noblemen and fashionable beauties of his day. His backgrounds of Antwerp blue clouds became characteritic of his work, and the long necks of the ladies prognosticate the Pre-Raphaelite girls. (Did Rossetti's use of gouache and stippling derive from the miniature artists?)

Cosway's greatest rival was George Engleheart (1750–1829), whose portraits of quiet dignity and restrained colouring contrasted with Cosway's dash and frivolity. Engleheart painted nearly 5,000 miniatures in nearly forty years, and they all have exquisite draughtsmanship and delicate colouring. He loved to dwell on texture and form of ribbons and feathers that decorated the high wigs of the times.

Other artists were John Smart, Ozias Humphry and Nathaniel and Andrew Plimer, to mention only a few. Ozias Humphry was one of the best and most prolific (1742–1810), being popular as an artist because he imparted an air of elegance and distinction to his sitters. He worked on paper as well as ivory, using crayon and watercolour in the style of Downman.

[1] Ivory was first used by Lens in 1708 in Britain, but in Italy in 1698 Rosalba Carriera incorporated portraits on ivory in *fondelli* (little boxes) which were popular all over Europe.

To return now to the general trend of landscape work: it must be remembered that the quiet colours of early watercolours were a deliberate choice, the artist following the fashion in oil-painting, which had at that time subdued tones and muted colours. The portraits of Lely and Van Dyck, worked up as they were on the under-painting of grey or terre verte, were very delicate in colouring. Something similar happened too in the watercolour schools: a grey or sepia undercoat served as a 'grisaille' and local colour was added in thin washes.

There were two main groups of artists in the eighteenth century: the followers of Paul Sandby, who were content with factual renderings of the scene; and another group who infused a

Sketch of a painting by Richard Wilson, which illustrates the classical method of composition. Background, foreground and middle distance are clearly defined. The large, dark tree and the pointing figures in the foreground, as well as the rod of the fisherman draw the eye towards the subject—the church in the middle distance. This is positioned in the 'Golden Section'. The lighting of the picture is also in the classical tradition, being parallel with the plane of the picture and coming from one direction. Most of these conventions can be seen in the work of eighteenth-century artists.

greater imaginative intensity into the topographical drawings.
They were all, however, greatly influenced by the continental
schools, notably Claude Lorrain, Poussin and Salvator Rosa,
using their ideals of pictorial composition and giving the English
scene a fashionable, Italianate atmosphere.

John Varley (Plate 1) followed the Sandby tradition. The
Sandby style of careful drawing in ink—he began as a military
draughtsman—with washes of colour added, can also be seen in
the works of Michelangelo Rooker (1743–1801) who delighted
in rendering the textures of brick and stone in old buildings; in
the drawings of Edward Dayes (1763–1804) with scenes of city
life, his elegant figures in well-conceived groups against architectural backgrounds. Thomas Girtin was a pupil of Dayes, but
his art soon outshone that of his master. With Francis Towne
and J. R. Cozens he opened new horizons for the watercolour in
Britain, and indeed in the world.

J. R. Cozens (1752–1797) did not follow his father Alexander,
who rarely coloured his pen and ink drawings (Plate 8). The
father had been a great experimenter, exploring the possibility
of making up a composition from a series of blots in sepia or
black ink. His rendering of mountains are spirited and rather
loose in style with a good deal of 'expression' in the straggly and
sinuous lines. His son, John Robert, although he used colour,
did so in a very modest way: dim blues, brownish greys and
greens formed the main ingredients of his palette; he delighted in
drawing lonely mountains and crevasses with a finely rendered
sky that have a majesty and breadth which are most fascinating.
He takes the viewer into his landscape, engulfing the spirit with a
deep feeling of the awesome loneliness of the wild places. The
artist's own melancholy nature found an echo, perhaps, in these
barren wastes and expressed the feeling of the romantic traveller
of the eighteenth century (Plate 9).

Another artist greatly moved by mountains was Francis Towne.
Walks in the Welsh hills, Italy and Switzerland gave him con-
genial subjects. His precision of line—he saw everything forming
a linear pattern—makes a balanced composition that catches even
the terror of perilous heights in a cage of lines. His best drawings

1. John Varley: *Landscape in North Wales*; watercolour and pen and ink.   *British Museum*

2. Thomas Rowlandson: *Villagers merry-making*; pen and ink and watercolour. *British Museum*

3. William Hamilton: *Girl at a Cottage Door*; watercolour and gouache.
Author's collection

4. Sir Joshua Reynolds: *Portrait Study*; pen and ink and watercolour. *Author's collection*

5. George Romney: *Figure Study*; pen and sepia wash. *Author's collection*

of Alpine scenes like *The Source of the Arveiron* and the view of Lake Como record the essence of the landscape with a fine selection of broad masses, expressing too the effect of light and shade. 'It is the distinction of Towne', writes Laurence Binyon,[1] 'that his mind is never content with the surface of things; it is their structural relations that he seeks to grasp' (Plate 7).

William Pars (1742–1782) gives a similar rendering, composes his pictures well, but he works with a cool understanding of the components of the landscape without being stirred himself or stirring the viewer. William Marlow (1740–1813) liked to draw country houses and castles with a partiality for Ludlow; his pen and ink and pencil lines are rather free and his colours wide in range, a quiet brown predominating. In the same vein are the drawings of John 'Warwick' Smith (1749–1831) whose colours, with a pale Prussian blue and greyish browns and greens, can be a little monotonous. He painted numerous Italian views, too, and is regarded by many as the forerunner of Girtin's style in his direct washes without preliminary underpainting of grey. He used the traditional methods, too, and did not break away entirely from the pen and ink outline referred to earlier.

It is Thomas Girtin in his short life (1775–1802) who transformed the watercolour in Britain, finally making the break with tradition, that demanded the ink or pencil outline, washed with pale colours over a monochrome rendering of the forms. Taking Canaletto perhaps as his model, he loved to explore wide vistas and achieved a serenity and breadth of vision unrivalled in English painting. He was a chronic asthmatic; perhaps he liked to breathe the pure air of these wide-open spaces to relieve his complaint and alleviate too a certain constriction of the spirit that this ailment brings. His *White House at Chelsea* (1800) in its economy of effect is a remarkable painting, by no means an accurate rendering of the scene but a perfect evocation of the evening light and atmosphere. Subtle variations of tone, combined with delicate drawing and a colour scheme of brownish green, ochre, light red and burnt sienna that predominate always in his palette, are

---

[1] *English Watercolours*, Laurence Binyon.

3*

entirely satisfactory; though it must be remembered that some of
the bright blue that he liked so much has probably faded from
many of his paintings.   The limited colours were, of course, of
his own choice.   There was a much larger range available, but
Girtin was content to explore the variations of tone in a very
few colours.   In his drawings one can recognize the peculiar
loops (like a Greek 'ε') at the ends of the pen and ink lines.
This form can be seen too in some of his brush-strokes.   The
direct washes he applied and the warm colour of his shadows were
a complete innovation (Plate 6).

John Constable, although primarily considered as a great
landscape painter in oils, also made many drawings of freshness
and vitality that make one wish he had produced more.   Under
Girtin's influence he was changed as he says 'from an amateur to a
painter'.   He captures the mood of the landscape in his sketches
of the Lake District.   Later he lightened his palette (and his
mood) and produced sparkling drawings of his beloved Stour
and Flatford, with an eye for the changing moods of skies,
observed by the knowing eye of the miller's lad.

Thomas Gainsborough's first love was landscape.   He con-
fessed to George III that he would have loved to devote all his
time to painting landscapes, but he had to make his living by
portraiture.   His pen and wash drawings on grey paper, heightened with white, have a feeling of air and light and a carefully
composed pattern, employing the triangular form of structure.
The feathery trees are entirely his own, seen again in many of the
backgrounds of his portraits.   The influence of Claude is obvious,
but it is a French elegance very much Englished into a view that
is essentially native.   Gainsborough's love of manipulating pieces
of rock, cauliflower and moss on his studio table to make up his
tree-forms contributed a novel touch to his modelling; but the
open-air feeling of his drawings could only have been achieved
by direct observation from nature.   His colour is very economic:
a pale wash of ochre or light red may suggest a pathway or a
shadowy dell, and it is enough to convey the scene (Plate 11).

Equally reticent in colour, perhaps in imitation of Gainsborough, are the drawings of Thomas Barker of Bath.   He was

born at Pontypool, but settled in Bath early in his career. His compositions have a dark, foreboding gloom and are sometimes a little affected, but I like his delicate drawing and subtle colouring (Plate 10). His pattern of tonal values is also well worth careful study and his figures are good and well placed.

Another artist of limited colour range was John Sell Cotman (1782–1842). His landscapes of Norwich and the justly famous *Greta Bridge* are made up of flat washes that leave out unessential details in order to achieve a balanced and harmonious composition. Many critics have pointed out that the disposition of the rocks in the painting is quite different from those in the river: it is the artist's own design that makes it into a masterpiece by his selection. He used an absorbent paper, which did not allow of much scrubbing and altering; the colourwash itself is a thing of beauty. Later his colouring became rather harsh in an attempt to render the light of Normandy and he explored the possibilities of painting with sour paste, which enriched his palette and textures; but it is the early works which are among the supreme masterpieces of British watercolours. Plate 12 is typical of his early work with its broad washes and seemingly careless blobs, combining subtlety with liveliness.

His son John Joseph followed similar methods. His *The Windmill in Marshland* in my collection (Plate 13) is all gold and blue, and the pen and ink drawing might have been done by the father, but the composition is a little shaky and the colours—with perhaps a little too much of the sour paste—rather chalky and heavy. Pencil sketches and pen and ink drawings by these artists often come up for sale and are well worth the few pounds they fetch.

Miles Edmund, the eldest son, has some very fine drawings, but his colouring and methods are so close to those of his father that it is sometimes difficult to tell them apart.

The Cotmans were, of course, prominent members of the 'Norwich School', and this seems an appropriate place to describe it. Norwich had always had affinities with the Netherlands, and, as thousands had emigrated to that part of England from the Low Countries in the sixteenth century, there was a blood kinship, too. They were inclined to look on nature and the landscape in the same way. Derek Clifford writes[1] 'The landscapes of Ruysdael, Van Goyen, Hobbema and Guyp, are the work of men who have quite a different relationship with the world about them than, for example, have Giorgione, Claude or Salvator Rosa. At root, they do not seek to use landscape for some human purpose, to establish a mood or to represent an ideal: their relationship is more humble, that of fellow-creatures in a beloved creation.'

Norwich painters were admired because they were of Norwich; their paintings should be bought from the 'heart rather than taste', wrote Sir Martin Shee in a poem celebrating their works. Eighteenth century taste explored the delights of the 'picturesque', —those rough, dramatic qualities of landscape, advocated by William Gilpin in his *Picturesque Tours*. Travel was difficult and arduous, so they sought the picturesque at home.

John Crome (1768–1821), apprenticed to a coachpainter, copied prints at the beginning of his career. His early work is in the eighteenth century manner of grey monochrome with colours added. They are direct and honest records of the scene with little attempt at picture-making in the manner of Gainsborough or Wilson. There is no striving after dramatic effect in his golden greens and browns and grey-blues, but the sketches have the quietness of authority and the lasting power of sincerity. The painting of young oaks in my collection is typical of his work with the spots of green and golden brown and intermediate tints.

Robert Ladbrooke (1770–1842) made many wash-drawings on blue paper. He liked strong, dark colours. His drawings are similar in technique to Crome's, but the washes are broader and the atmosphere more gloomy.

Other members of the Norwich circle are John Thirtle (1777–1839), Robert Dixon (1780–1815), Henry Ninham (1795–1874), James Stark (1794–1859), George Vincent (1796–1831), Robert Leman (1799–1863), Thomas Lound (1802–1861) Samuel Colkett (1800–1863) Henry Bright (1810–1873), Joseph Stannard 1797–1830).

[1] *The Norwich School*, Derek Clifford.

Thirtle, Bright and Dixon are the most prominent. Thirtle worked as a frame-maker and painter of miniatures. He paints in the manner of Peter de Wint, in pure wash technique with a predominantly warm palette. He also used to wash over his pictures with a large brush to give the effect of granulation.

Robert Dixon was at first a scene-painter. His pictures are broadly conceived, rather theatrical in manner, with strong purples and deep greys.

Henry Ninham had a liking for cottages and inns with greens and browns as the main colours His works are modest and not without charm. John Berney Crome, eldest son of John Crome, specialized in moonlit scenes which found a ready market and became his regular output as an artist.

James Stark developed a new approach in his use of direct washes of clear colours; but his use of tinted papers rather detracted from the brightness of the washes. His sketches of trees are his most happy ones, and I have one of his country scenes near Newbury which is quite fresh and lovely.

George Vincent painted in Scotland as well as in Norwich and his pictures are unaffected and competent without introducing any startling innovations.

Joseph Stannard (1797-1830) was a painter of seascapes as well as landscapes. His pencil or chalk drawings with slight washes are also enlivened with well-drawn figures, remarkable enough in the Norwich school, where the figures are sometimes barely competent!

There were dozens of others who painted, including a host of amateurs, for drawing and painting were accomplishments specially cultivated in the Norwich of those days. Eloise Stannard, wife of Joseph Stannard, produced large numbers of dainty flowerpieces and still-lives and survived her husband by fifty years. Thomas Lound showed the influence of David Cox in his addiction to built-up, criss-cross strokes of the brush. He imitated many others too (he was an avid collector and could not resist showing his knowledge!) and his colouring varied a good deal in quality.

Colkett worked in the manner of Stark and the early Constable.

The brothers William and John Cantiloe Joy loved to paint the sea, often working together on the same picture; their peagreen ships on leaden waves have an authentic tang. The Rev. E. T. Daniell was a gifted amateur with occasionally good draughtsmanship and quiet and tasteful colour.

Henry Bright took lessons from John Sell Cotman and B. Crome and was closely connected with Norwich at the beginning of his career. He was a competent draughtsman always and his technique embraced the use of chalk, gouache, watercolour and even gummed washes—sometimes all mixed together. The results are startling and sometimes successful. They were popular in his day and he made a fortune. The chalk drawings date from 1828–1840, the gouache from about 1841, and he practised pure watercolour all the while, sometimes using a grey Scotch paper, heightened with gouache.

4. The Nineteenth Century

THE Watercolour Society was founded in 1804, and henceforth the public had an opportunity to see regular exhibitions of the members' works. The young John Constable wrote: 'The mechanism of painting is their delight. Execution is their chief aim' and in many respects this was a just criticism.

The painters had everything in the way of technique—everything except largeness of spirit. The public expected 'finish' and dexterity, and watercolour painting deteriorated because it 'substituted an external for an internal standard and the communication of facts for the communication of emotion' (Laurence Binyon).[1]

Among the founders of the Watercolour Society was John Varley (1778–1842), who had a long career as an artist and produced a vast quantity of landscapes, competent but rather vapid. His smaller drawings I find full of spirit and much more vigorous than his 'finished' works. His pupil, William Henry Hunt, acquired the name of 'Bird's Nest' Hunt because of his liking for this subject in a still-life painting and his dexterity in rendering the details of straw, moss and feathers.[2] He also painted landscapes and portraits of real charm and evolved a style of pure washes with the addition of minute details in body-colour which was quite his own. Another pupil of John Varley was Copley Fielding (1787–1853) who had an occasionally happy touch and a feeling for space in his seascapes. The most promising of Varley's pupils was William Turner, called 'William Turner of Oxford' to avoid confusion with his greater namesake. Some of his drawings of woodland scenes were of great sensitivity and full of atmosphere

[1] *English Watercolours.*
[2] His preliminary wash of Chinese white probably had a little gum to prevent the ground from 'lifting'.

in his younger days. *Wychwood Forest* at the South Kensington Museum is superb with its darkling menace of ancient trees.

Peter de Wint carried on the tradition of Girtin and Cotman. His sombre landscapes of his beloved Lincoln in russets and warm yellows and greens, once seen, can never be forgotten. With mostly blank skies, they are reposeful and quiet in tone, tenderly painted with well-drawn and well-placed figures. My own *Three Figures on a Footbridge* is typical of his work, full of soft, autumnal colouring. (He painted most of his landscapes in summer and early autumn, because this was the time of year when he had most leisure as a teacher.) The dark washes are luminous and rich, the result of direct painting, which is the secret of his power and charm. Some washes are superimposed, too; the round blobs on foliage and pathways are reminiscent of Girtin. Ochre, burnt sienna, umber and indigo form the main colours of de Wint's palette, and his liking for long, horizontal lines in his landscapes may recall his Dutch ancestry. Many of his drawings doubtlessly looked bluer when first painted; the indigo he loved so much has faded, leaving the Indian red predominant with its warm glow.

These artists were tied to the landscape they loved. Others, like Samuel Palmer, John Linnell (1792–1882) and Edward Calvert (1799–1883), imposed their own vision of life—a religious or rather, mystical evocation of 'something far more deeply interfused'—on to the landscape, no less loved, but a symbol of their beliefs rather than a topographical recording of the scene. Palmer was greatly influenced by Blake, but was no mere imitator; the spark 'seemed but to kindle the fuel which flamed in early drawings such as *Ruth* and his later drawings of Shoreham.' His drawings were out of key with the times (1825); his 'valley of vision' was ridiculed by the critics; the figures were out of proportion, the blossoms too large, the blazing colour—pure poetry in paint to us—far in advance of his age. He used a complicated technique, using a variety of pens, the crow-quill, the reed, and saucers full of colour, which he had prepared before hand so that some of the colour 'set'. He then applied these colours very freely with a two-inch wide brush, painting with a broad sweep.

He appears to have used gum, or this may be the accumulated honey or glycerine in the paint, as some passages look shiny. Plate 17 shows a typical painting.

John Linnell's drawings have something of a similar mystic approach to landscape, akin to Blake's sinuous line. Indeed, one might almost say that their landscapes were composed in the same way as Blake made up his figure-compositions; not by making a faithful delineation of the model, but working by some kind of inner compulsion that imposed its own rhythms on the subject and expressed the artist's personal emotions: it was 'expressionist' in the sense that they portrayed their inner visions and conflicts rather than the configurations of the landscape.

John Linnell enjoyed the patronage of Benjamin West and Dr. Monro and painted many landscapes in watercolour of Windsor and its environs, as well as others in North Wales. I have one of these in my collection, which shows an economy of line and just a suggestion of colour.

But I have said nothing so far about the man at whose feet this little band of visionaries sat and comforted his old age with their kindness and affectionate interest. It is difficult to deal adequately with the work of William Blake in a few short paragraphs. So rich in imaginative power is his work ('damned good to steal from', said Fuseli!) and so complex in its diversity, so deeply interfused too with his poetic works and his prophetic books that it is difficult to isolate the paintings.

Born in 1757, he was solitary and lonely even as a boy and saw a vision of angels in a tree when he was eight: the vision stayed with him all his life, and it is this power of seeing other-worldly beings that makes his drawings so strange and appealing in a way that no other artist can. He bought prints of the works of Raphael and Michelangelo, and these, together with the antique casts acquired by his father, gave him a deep and life-long love of the heroic figures that he later reproduced in his own drawings. He never used a model, but gained his anatomical knowledge from his work as an engraver and copyist of ancient monuments. Martin Hardie quotes Hosea in a final word on Blake's quality: 'I have used similitudes'.

His technique of drawing was complicated: he engraved the outlines and then applied watercolour, retaining some drawings for sale separately from the printed books; he used washes of glue as well as ink, which gave a mottled appearance. He also used what he called 'fresco', which consisted of watercolour on a plaster ground of whiting and glue, laid on canvas or linen; an intriguing craquelure appears in these paintings. Direct water-colour can be seen in some of his drawings, too. He had his own peculiar method of representing fire and flame, which seemed to fascinate him. All his drawings, however, still used the ink outline as a framework, employing the wash of monochrome colour as well to suggest volume. His numerous illustrations of the Bible and of Dante all employ this method: the line is lyrical and flowing, expressing the mood rather than the letter of the text (Plate 18). A close study of Blake's drawings is most rewarding; one discovers new riches, new complexities of linear rhythm, new delicacies of colour: all bound together by a most powerful vision.

Quite different in feeling, though somewhat similar in style, were Calvert's illustrations—one can hardly call them landscapes. He was reputed to be 'pagan' and had an altar to Pan in his back-garden. He seems to have reverted also to the eighteenth-century style of drawing; his *Primitive City* with its clear pen and ink outlines and light tints is almost like an illumination, but points forward too, in its minute detail and delicate colouring, to the Pre-Raphaelites.

Another who sat at the feet of Blake was F. O. Finch (1802–1862) also a pupil of Varley, exhibiting his first pictures at the Royal Academy when he was fifteen. Strongly influenced by Claude, he could on occasion break away and produce pictures of a great finish, something like George Barrett's in style. He used the same trick of wiping out the high-lights on the foliage.

George Barrett (Jun.) (1767–1842) belonged to an earlier age, but it was only at the beginning of the nineteenth century that he produced his best work. His pictures are in the style of Claude with an expanse of landscape melting into a distant horizon with cattle or figures on a shadowed foreground, the sky being of palest amber and blue. In his book, *Theory and Practice of Watercolour Painting*, he defends his method of painting directly without an undercoat of grey. His palette consisted of yellow ochre, burnt sienna, light red, pink madder, cobalt and Indian yellow—a predominance of warm colours. Later in his career he produced highly-coloured landscapes.

William Havell (1782–1857) came into prominence about the same time. He belonged to a family of artists, his brothers being engravers, and was greatly influenced by Varley and David Cox. His landscapes have great breadth of vision, particularly skilful in showing the effect of sunshine on distant hills. Many of his drawings, eminently suitable because of their meticulous detail, were used as subjects for engravings. He visited China, Calcutta and Italy, making numerous studies. His Welsh landscape in my own collection shows a castle and a wooded hillside under a sunset sky. The colours are sombre with some gouache in the crescent moon and the red cloak of a horseman in the foreground. His *Kilgerran Castle* is similar in treatment, though the sky is clearer. I think he deserves a better place among watercolour artists than he has at present. Perhaps the scarcity of his pictures accounts for this neglect.

Richard Parkes Bonington (1802–1837), though short-lived, exerted tremendous influence on painters in England. As a boy he copied Flemish landscapes in the Louvre, then sketched from nature, filling his notebooks with figures and colour notes and exhibited successfully both watercolours and oils. He came to England in 1825 on a short visit, and his works were so popular that many imitators sprang up. His brilliant, almost crude colours, captured the public taste. He used body-colour with the high-lights scraped out; another trick of his was to drag the brush across a previous wash, leaving broken colour. Rough paper was ideal for this effect. He also liked to varnish his drawings to emulate the richness and depth of oils, which were usually shown in the same exhibition. His pencil studies of costume, armour and architecture are lively and full of detail, though his perspective may be a little shaky. This often gives a clue to a genuine Bonington drawing.

An artist whose work is sometimes mistaken for Bonington's is Thomas Shotter Boys (1803–1874). He illustrated *Picturesque Architecture in Paris, Ghent, Antwerp and Rouen*, followed in 1842 by *Original Views of London as it is*. His townscapes are full of animated figures and his perspective always correct. His main colours are brownish greys and greens with an occasional accent of bright red in the manner of Bonington. He signed his drawings 'T. B.' or 'T. S. B.', placing these initials in unexpected places such as the sides of boxes, carts or paving-stones. The dragged-brush technique was his favourite trick to render textures.

Another artist influenced by Bonington was John Scarlett Davis (1804–1845), a native of Leominster. He painted portraits, landscapes and architectural interiors in oils as well as in water-colours, his interiors being atmospheric and invariably well-drawn. He used pen and sepia wash as well as pure watercolour; the grouping and lighting of his figures are well-contrived and full of human interest.

I conclude this chapter with two of the giants of watercolour painting: Joseph Mallord William Turner (1775–1851) and David Cox (1783–1859).

It is impossible to deal in a few short paragraphs with all of Turner's *œuvre*, executed during a long and active career. Even as a boy he loved to sketch from nature, and it is this habit of going directly to the scene and storing up in his memory details of colours, form, light and atmosphere that gives his work a richness and infinite variety of texture and tint. He could also retain in his memory a feeling for the scene and reproduce it at will. Many of his drawings were made twenty or thirty years after he had visited the scene. He began as a factual recorder, almost in the style of Dayes and Varley. Four small sepia drawings in my collection (part of his *Liber Studiorum*) are exquisitely done as a guide to the tyro in the rudiments of composition. Another of his early drawings has pale blue ink in the background and brown in the foreground (Plate 19), another method of the early topographical artists.

By 1799, however, his style had already begun to assume that atmospheric quality that we admire so much. Farington notes in his *Diary* (February 9th, 1799) 'He has no systematic process for making drawings. By washing and occasionally rubbing out, he at last expresses in some degree the idea in his mind.' (Another artist called this method 'fudging it out).[1] In 1802 in a tour of Switzerland, he used opaque colour. A few years later he developed the technique of washing out colour, lifting out light with a rag or wet brush and even scraping out with a knife or rubbing with bread or sandpaper. Other washes are then floated on to give richness or subtle effects of light, and a dry brush sometimes adds touches of colour. The final effect is one of incomparable richness and subtlety (Plate 20).

John Constable at first did not like his paintings because they were not 'true to nature', but later, on seeing Turner's paintings at the Academy in 1828, he called them 'golden visions, glorious and beautiful; they are only visions, but still they are art, and one could live or die with such paintings'. And Hazlitt called him 'the ablest landscape painter now living'. It is light that he painted, the light on mountain peaks, on lagoons and rivers and in the sky; sunset was a favourite theme, giving him scope for his symphonies of scarlets and golds and yellows with smouldering shadows on rock and cloud, so that the objects themselves seem to dissolve in a maelstrom of drifting flame.

His pencil sketches during the last years of his life are economical of colour, with only faint washes over the outlines to suggest the scene: red or blue or ochre, with a good deal of the white paper showing. I conclude with the words of an eminent critic: 'In the course of his long life he produced a far larger corpus of work than any artist in history. While other artists have struggled with failure of energy, paucity of subjects and poverty of ideas, his labour lay in making a choice among infinite riches. . . . What puts Turner in a class by himself is that he never seems to have experienced failure and always to have lived and worked in a spirit of inspiration, often ecstatic inspiration.'[2]

A lesser giant and a close follower in many aspects of his art was David Cox (1783–1859) who began life as a scene-painter in

[1] W. H. Hunt.
[2] Martin Hardie: *Watercolour Painting in Britain.*

Birmingham and Swansea. His early sketches in sepia were traditional, but he soon began to appreciate the effects of light on land and sky and, after taking a teaching post in Hereford Grammar School, published his *Treatise on Landscape Painting and Effect in Watercolours* in 1814, illustrated with his own drawings made into etchings. Cox maintained that 'The principal art of landscape painting consists in conveying to the mind the most forcible effect which can be produced from the various classes of scenery; which possesses the power of exciting an interest superior to that resulting from any other effect; and which can only be obtained by a judicious selection of particular tints, and a skilful arrangement and application of them to differences in time, seasons and situations.' He recommended gamboge, light ochre, light red, lake, vermilion, burnt sienna, Vandyke brown, Prussian blue, indigo, black and sepia—a very wide range of colours—but in practice we find that he limits himself to only a few of these in his own paintings. Later he substituted cobalt for Prussian blue.

He made many sketching excursions to various parts of Britain and the Continent, producing innumerable drawings and paintings, which sold well. His style developed from a rather dry and precise imitation of Varley to a looser, more atmospheric rendering. His colour became bolder, and he used broken brush-strokes, often criss-crossing diagonally to produce the flickering light of passing clouds, or storms on the heath. At the end of his long life he produced the pictures we value most today, many of them made on the greyish 'Scotch' paper he liked so much though Ruskin doubted whether the 'loose and blotted handling' was altogether successful, but concludes that 'what there is of accidental in his mode of reaching it, answers gracefully to the accidental part of nature herself.'[1] Although the public demanded finished works—and he supplied them—it is the sketchy ones that we admire most today, especially his renderings of lonely moors and mountains. He was a master of the direct wash; limpid colour flowed from his brush; but he could exert all the subtleties of flickering brush-strokes, dragged dry-brush and

[1] *Modern Painters*, Vol. 1.

scraping and washing out, if the atmosphere demanded it (Plate 16).

But it was not only landscape that occupied the artists of the nineteenth century. We must now look at the figure painters, the animal-lovers and the illustrators, not forgetting the Neo-Classicists.

5. The Neo-Classicists

I WOULD like to devote a short chapter to this side of watercolour painting and drawing, because it is, I feel, a branch of art
too often neglected in an appraisal of the work being done
in Britain not only in the eighteenth and nineteenth centuries but
before this time. (See '*Venus and Adonis*' by G. Kneller, Plate 22).

Sir James Thornhill, whose designs can be seen at Greenwich
and in the murals in the dome of Saint Paul's, left a large number
of drawings in sepia and pen and ink which are attractive enough
to be included in any collection. I have one called *A Group of
the Gods* (Plate 21), which, though small—little more than some
eight inches by six—has a good deal to recommend it. The
drawing of the mythological figures is lively, the line is expressive
with a nervous energy that seems lacking in his more grandiose
works. Perhaps the inspiration evaporated when translated into
those massive murals! Be that as it may, I would recommend
this and similar drawings to the collector who wants to have
something different from the dreary, second-rate De Wint's and
David Coxes that so often grace the walls of the modest collector.
Drawings make up in liveliness what they lack in the siren charms
of colour, and the manipulation of pen or pencil seems to catch
something of the artist's personality as it grapples with the pro-
blem of recording the idea in visible form.

The ancient gods were, after all, personifications of feelings and
ideas, if not ideals. and their resurrection by modern artists is
not a cultural foible: they stood for very real states of mind. They
are only 'illustrations', scoffs the modern critic; but one may ask:
what is less creative about such a work than a landscape or a
still-life, or an abstract? All demand skill of hand and eye, a
sense of balance, a taste for colour, the ability to orchestrate the
elements of drawing and design into a pleasant and coherent

6. Thomas Girtin: *Kirkstall Abbey*; watercolour.   *Victoria & Albert Museum*

7. Francis Towne: *Valle Crucis Abbey*; watercolour.   *By permission of the National Museum of Wales*

8. Alexander Cozens: *Landscape with Bridge and Cattle*; pen and black ink. *British Museum*

9. J. R. Cozens: *Extensive View of a River flowing into the Sea through a wooded Valley*; watercolour. *Author's collection*

10. Thomas Barker of Bath: *The Mill in the Mountains*; watercolour. *Author's collection*

11. Thomas Gainsborough: *The Old Cottage*; pen and grey ink, grey wash on grey paper, heightened with white. *Author's collection*

12. J. S. Cotman: *Landscape with river and Cattle*; watercolour. *Victoria & Albert Museum*

13. John Joseph Cotman: *The Windmill in Marshland*; watercolour and gouache. *Author's collection*

14. John Glover: *Landscape with Bridge*; watercolour. *Author's collection*

15. Peter de Wint: *Three Figures on a Footbridge*; watercolour. *Author's collection*

16. David Cox: *Wooded River and flock of sheep*; watercolour. *Author's collection*

17. Samuel Palmer: *In a Shoreham Garden*; watercolour and gouache.
Victoria & Albert Museum

18. William Blake: *Christ Trampling down Satan*; pen and ink and watercolour. *By permission of the National Museum of Wales*

whole.   And is reverence for past glories altogether a bad thing? Poetic truths are eternal.

An interest in the antique in the second half of the eighteenth century and the beginning of the nineteenth spread throughout all the arts.   Although Gainsborough and Reynolds withdrew from the ranks of the 'historical' painters, there were still many artists of considerable merit left to hold the field.

Shaftesbury, in his *Characteristics* of 1711, claimed that art is governed by rational rules not by uncontrolled feelings, and to create beauty the artist must unite order and harmony and must seek inspiration in the works of ancient, classical masters and of the moderns like Raphael and Poussin.   The 'Grand Tour' and numerous guide-books to Italy and Greece, added fuel to the flame; a number of archaeological excavations brought to light new 'finds', which were taken home as souvenirs.   Sir William Hamilton's Greek vases influenced the art of Flaxman and Fuseli as well as providing subjects for the pottery of Josiah Wedgwood and the architectural embellishments of the brothers Adam.

Greek statuary inspired many artists, who imitated the poses and gestures, and also the classic costume of the ancient heroes even when depicting the soldiers and admirals of the day!   James Barry (1741–1806) used classical statues such as the torso Belvedere and the Farnese Hercules and settings from Salvator Rosa for his historical paintings, the most famous being the series that decorate the walls of the Royal Society of Arts in the Adelphi, London.

Henry Fuseli (1741–1825) was of Swiss origin and settled in London in 1764.   He had a profound knowledge of Homer and illustrated many themes from the Iliad and the Odyssey.   He advocated, however, and himself practised an individual 'expression' of emotions which he saw in the ancients.   Fantastic and horrific aspects of human suffering he excelled in; his sprawling, gesticulating figures appear to have an almost superhuman strength; sometimes they are ridiculous, but often they have a strange power to move.   His landscape backgrounds are sketchy, his colouring often crude; pink and poisonous green washes overlap, and it is the strong lines of pen and brush that hold our attention.   His drawings in pen, pencil and crayon are most

4*

attractive and may be bought usually for under a hundred pounds.

Benjamin West (1738–1820), a Pennsylvanian, followed Fuseli as President of the Royal Academy and was the most prolific history painter of his age, being much revered by his contemporaries. General esteem for his paintings has cooled rather today; we can see the ghost of Poussin and the classic antique statues parading too obviously; but his drawings from the living model in pen and ink and sepia wash or in grey ink are vigorous and sensitive (Plate 23). They can be bought in the salerooms for about sixty pounds.

Angelica Kauffmann (1741–1807) also produced many watercolour drawings illustrating antique subjects. Her portraits and figure compositions have a strong whiff of the ancient about them, but are not without charm. They are sometimes a little sentimental, but are quiet and tender in colouring and have the graceful lines of their age.

Echoes of Michelangelo and Raphael appear in the works of Giovanni Battista Cipriani (1727–1785) whose numerous ink and wash drawings appear from time to time. They are rather derivative although the line is sensitive and lively.

John Flaxman (1755–1826) was most famous for his monuments. He produced a great number of preliminary sketches in ink and wash, which in their flowing line and exuberant feeling excite more admiration today than his coldly classical statuary. His drawings may be little more than outlines, but the outlines have the refined grace and simplicity of the figures on a Greek vase (Plate 24).

George Romney (1734–1802), celebrated as a portrait-painter and enamoured of his immortal Emma, produced many sketches in pen and ink and wash, illustrating classical themes. Some of his figure studies for portraits also have a 'classic' simplicity and grace of linear design (Plate 5).

John Hamilton Mortimer (1741–1779) was adored by the students for his skill in drawing the male figure, a skill he used well in his illustrations of classical stories. His sepia wash drawing of *Hercules and Anteas* in my collection is a good example of his style, showing delicate modelling of the figures, combined with graceful outline in a good composition that repays careful study (Plate 25).

Amos Green and his brother James are little known water-colour artists. I have one of Amos's drawings, which illustrates the 'Origin of Painting', a favourite theme among the Neo-classic artists: a young girl traces the outline of her lover's profile on the wall. The colouring of rose-pink and pale greens and golds is rather sentimental, but one must still admire the competence of the composition.

William Edward Frost (1810–1877) brings the movement to a belated end in the nineteenth century. His watercolour drawing of *Young Bacchus* in my collection is more like a young cockney newsvendor, dressed (or rather undressed) for the occasion, but the drawing and colouring are vigorous with a good deal of subtlety in the modelling.

Sir Edward Coley Burne-Jones (1833–1898), Dante Gabriel Rossetti (1828–1882) and Sir L. Alma-Tadema (Plate 28) occasionally illustrated the legends of Greece and Rome, but bathed all in the unreal light of their own imaginations to such an extent that one forgets the legend and admires the poetic colouring in the rather hothouse atmosphere of the *fin de siècle*. The drooping maidens and yearning young men are far from the robustness of Greek statuary; only the line is there and the ideal anatomy. Burne-Jones could, however, produce some drawings of great vigour, which I much prefer to his 'finished' studio paintings. I have an *Ixion* in gouache, which he never used for a larger painting perhaps because of the nudity of the youth lashed to the wheel. *Phyllis and Demophoon* (Plate 26) got the artist into trouble when first exhibited. He was asked to obliterate the boy's pubic hair, but withdrew the painting instead and resigned from the Old Watercolour Society in protest.

G. F. Watts (1817–1904), Lord Leighton (1830–1896) and J. W. Waterhouse (1847–1917) produced many illustrations of Greek legend in oils, and made many studio sketches from life as preliminary drawings of figures and drapery.

G. F. Watts was a painter and sculptor; he painted allegorical subjects such as *Love and Life* and also carried out large frescoes in the Houses of Parliament and Lincoln's Inn; he was preoccupied with the power of love and the fear of death, which he allegorized in his works. His figure studies turn up occasionally and are meticulously drawn with excellent knowledge of anatomy.

Lord Leighton also produced many works dealing with Greek Mythology, his most famous painting shows *Hercules Fighting Death*, the figure of Hercules being particularly well observed, no doubt from the living model.

J. W. Waterhouse also shows good figure work and imaginative use of colour. Every schoolboy knows his *The Lady of Shalott*, and *Hylas and the Nymphs*, which exemplify his fine use of colour. The figures are also well-drawn, and there is a searching sense of character and otherworldliness about the dreamy faces of the nymphs and the ill-fated Lady of Shalott. I have come across many of his drawings; they are worth looking out for, and are fairly cheap at the moment.

Simeon Solomon (1840–1905) also illustrated religious and mystical themes with a special line in Angels and Spirits. A few of his drawings in red chalk have come into the salerooms lately and are well worth collecting. They are a little like Burne-Jones's work in their swan-necked beauties and large, shadowed eyes— even the boys look too good to be true—but have the nostalgic charm of a vanished age.

There are echoes of the Greek legends among the moderns too; Michael Ayrton has used the story of Icarus in his sculptures and has many preliminary sketches on the theme in pencil and pen and ink, drawn directly from the male nude in his own semi-abstracted style. Keith Vaughan also draws male nudes in pencil (Plate 35), pen and ink and gouache, some of them illustrating the classic stories and again using a semi-abstract style; but he has some pencil studies made early in his career which are more realistic. I have one in my collection, which is quite near to the living model and shows an affectionate interest in the details of anatomy, akin to the French drawings of male nudes of the eighteenth century. These can be bought for twenty or thirty pounds now, but may be worth very much more in a few years' time when admiration for figure studies returns among collectors and the public.

6. The Animal-Lovers

THE British have always been a nation of animal-lovers; and this shows in the pictures they buy; artists have subscribed to this taste by making careful studies of the horse, the dog, in fact all the animals that one sees about the house and the farm and the country estate.

George Stubbs (1724–1806) comes to mind at once with his life-long study of equine anatomy; and his influence is apparent in the graceful creatures that adorn the canvases of Fernely, Alken, Sturgess and George Morland.

George Morland's drawings in crayon and charcoal, lightly washed with watercolour, are charming evocations of the country scene in the eighteenth century. Groups of rustics posed outside country taverns, in or near stables and farms, are obviously drawn from life; one can almost smell the manure on their boots. His stockily-built men and his plump and rosy girls serving ale or hanging out the washing are easily recognized; his peculiar curly line in the foliage, and the gnarled branches of the trees are quite individual. I have two of his drawings in my collection. His sketches in pen, pencil or chalk are relatively cheap and are honest records of country life.

Another artist who loved to show animals as the main subject—in fact, often the only subject—of his drawings was Samuel Howitt, (1756–1822). He illustrated, or at least engravings were made from his drawings for, *The British Sportsman*, 1812 and *The Fables of Aesop* in the previous year. His animal studies are lively and accurate and show an affectionate interest in the idiosyncrasies of the creatures. Dogs, foxes, deer, horses are shown as they really are, not with some sentimental straining after effect, as in the pictures of Landseer ! *Stag Attacked by Hounds*, a signed drawing in my collection, I bought for ten pounds a few years ago. The brown ink outlines are sensitively drawn, though the colouring of burnt sienna and Prussian blue and green may not please everyone (Plate 31).

Henry Alken (1784–1850?) won fame as a designer of sporting prints and drawings. He does not seem to have made his drawings from sight, as none of his friends knew the identity of the artist who signed himself 'Ben Tally Ho'. His early work was in pure watercolour over a light pencil drawing; later he used direct washes and stronger colour. His horses are rather graceful, but the riders are solidly astride their steeds, obviously drawn by a man used to the saddle himself and a lover of the countryside and the open-air life. The skies and landscape backgrounds are pleasant and fresh.

Of quite a different class is Robert Hills (1769–1844) (Plate 29), whose drawings of cattle are among the finest of their kind; he evolved a peculiar style of colouring, using warm greens and golden yellows and browns, applied with a delicate, stippling touch that is quite individual. Like Stubbs, Hills applied himself to a careful study of anatomy: his sketch-books contain numerous drawings of deer, oxen, sheep and cattle. His etchings of animals, issued from 1798–1815, totalled 780. He liked to portray deer in their natural settings. Windsor Park and the Lake District are faithfully recorded. Many of his smaller sketches of groups of cattle are well within the reach of the modest collector. So are the drawings of Sawrey Gilpin (1762–1843), whose horses are accurately and affectionately observed in rural settings (Plate 30).

James Ward (1769–1859) also produced landscape and animal studies in the style of his brother-in-law George Morland and many of his preliminary sketches show superb draughtsmanship. His landscapes in pure watercolour are rare but worth looking out for; so are his figure-studies. I have one in my collection of an orange girl, most delicately drawn. His drawings are signed with the initials 'J. W.', sometimes 'J. W. R. A.' He was elected R.A. in 1811, but confused many collectors by adding the 'R. A.' to earlier drawings, irrespective of their actual date of composition.

Many paintings of animals were produced, too, by the Williams family, too numerous to mention individually. They are competent and realistic, without being particularly inspiring as works of art. I like their preliminary sketches best; they are full of careful observation and remind one of the cows of Cuyp, sitting placidly and solidly in their natural setting.

Other artists who specialised in cattle were T. S. and Henry Cooper. Their pencil and sepia sketches are comparatively cheap in the folios and show a sensitive appreciation of bovine beauty. Field and farmyard are affectionately recorded.

I cannot close this chapter without mentioning Joseph Crawhall (1861–1913) whose drawings often made on silk or linen, specially prepared by sizing—have the sweeping line and economical colour of Japanese paintings. Crawhall drew from memory with the cave-man's eye for essential details; but he had a decorative sense, too, that made his drawings more than just accurate delineations of animals: there is something of Picasso's legerdemain in their cunning.

7. The Illustrators

'**P**ICTURESQUE Cattermoles'[1] were being hung in the Water Colour Society's Exhibitions year after year in the first half of the nineteenth century; and one cannot dismiss all his work with derision. His paintings, without achieving any great heights, have a sincerity and competence, which pleased the public. I have one in my collection, illustrating some story of the Middle Ages with men in armour and a hall, well drawn. He uses liquid washes and some body-colour in the highlights (or as the catalogues put it 'Heightened with white').

Richard Westall (1765–1836) illustrated scenes from the Bible and classical legend, placing his figures in a beautifully composed landscape. One discerns the influence of Claude and Poussin in the delicate colouring and the rather artificial poses of the girls. I have in my collection a small illustration by him of Christ walking on the water. Although only a tiny drawing—little more than five by three inches, it is full of an austere light, and its limited colour scheme of ochre, light red and palest green adequately suggests the mystery of the holy subject. I have also a farmyard scene by this artist. The colour scheme is similar, but the drawing and the darker tones of byre and farmyard, give the impression that it was painted from sight. The range of his art is therefore not to be despised. His figures are always gracefully drawn in pencil or pale ink.

Joshua Cristall (1767–1847), also illustrated classical legends. Even as a boy he painted the whitewashed walls of his bedroom with a solution of liquorice, and his passion for figure-drawing led him eventually to scenes of rustic life, where he found the models for his pictures. Almost five hundred of his works were exhibited

[1] *Athenaeum*, 1839.

in the Water Colour Society's Exhibitions, all showing the artist's well-observed peasant girls at their domestic tasks, fisherfolk and farmers.   He exemplified Benjamin West's aphorism that 'Artists ought to represent their own Country as it is, and not represent that of which they could only have an idea.'[1]

Thomas Bewick (1753–1828) was a wood-engraver, who illustrated such books as *History of Quadrupeds* and *British Birds*, but he made many watercolour drawings as preparations for the engravings.   Some drawings of birds and flying fish can be seen at the Victoria & Albert Museum, and there are many of the original studies for the engravings in indian ink, washed with colour, at the British Museum.   Rural incidents are also illustrated, all distinguished by a fine line and sensitive exploration of character as well as faithful renderings of the country scene.

Another prolific illustrator was Thomas Stothard (1757–1834) who worked in pen and ink and monchrome washes in the early part of his career.   He also used pencil and watercolour and imitated the style of Mortimer in his shading with fine lines and dots.   Raphael and Watteau he admired very much, and his work shows their influence in figure-drawing and composition. He liked to add touches of white 'body-colour' to 'heighten' the highlights, a method much favoured by continental artists. Alphonese Legros used it later in his landscapes and figure studies.

Battle scenes were the delight of John Augustus Atkinson (1775–1831), and he illustrated a book dealing with costumes of Great Britain and the story of Don Quixote.

The caricaturists must now be mentioned: Bunbury, Gillray, Woodward and Dighton.   The first was an amateur of no great talent.   His drawings in pen and ink and sepia washes are lively and satirical in a mild sort of way, but we do not relish their humour very much these days: the point is lost on us.   His sketch of the Devil playing a fiddle may have amused the *haut monde*, who no doubt recognized the violinist being satirized, but later viewers are unmoved.

James Gillray (1757–1815) was a savage and angry artist.   His political cartoons in black chalk, red ink or pen and pencil, would

[1] Farington's Diary, 1808.

probably have landed him in gaol today. His work, because of its acrimony, has been compared to the writings of Swift. His illustration of *Cymon and Iphigenia* shows a coarse old man ogling a drunken girl, neither of whom are particularly good-looking; but one cannot help admiring the spirited drawing and the expressive gestures of the love-sick old dotard.

G. M. Woodward (1760–1809) drew many of his satires to please himself. It is difficult to conceive of his seven-foot high cartoon being made for publication. He also liked to divide his paper into compartments (like the 'houses' of a medieval play perhaps?) to illustrate different facets of the story of virtue wronged, repentant drunkards, etc. His men and women have thick, dark faces with blotchy complexions, competently drawn in profile but not so happy full-face. He liked adding bright, florid colours like crimson, yellow and emerald green to his ink outlines. One such in my collection shows a dinner party upset by a lady ringing the bell. The snarling dog, diagonally flung limbs, table-cloth and dishes make a busy and humorous tableau of confusion.

More gentle is the satire of Robert Dighton (1752–1814). His drawing of *A Windy Day* at the Victoria & Albert Museum shows a keen eye and a skilful hand; the ladies' hats, the bald man losing his wig, the flying petticoats, the fish and fruit on the road all contribute to a composition full of movement and bustle. Coloured washes, clean and harmonious, enliven the flowing lines and make this a very good watercolour indeed.

The best of the caricaturists was of course Thomas Rowlandson, who produced such a huge body of work that it is impossible to do justice to him in three short paragraphs. He was a veritable Turner among the cartoonists of the day; nothing escaped his attention; fashionable routs, market days, the foibles of high society in Bath, the meet, the seaside crowds—all received the comments of his flickering pen, some flattering, some critical, all graced with that free and flowing line of which he was a master. Colour did not interest him particularly; a pale wash of ochre or blue or green sometimes adds to the atmosphere, but it is the line that we are aware of most. Although many of his drawings are coarse and offensive, we should remember Hazlitt's aphorism that 'the Greatest grossness sometimes accompanies the greatest refinement, as a natural relief, one to the other' and realize that an age that could stomach cock-fights, the goring of dogs in bull-baiting and public executions could also see the comical side of brutality, or perhaps enjoy it for its own sake. Martin Hardie calls this side of Rowlandson's art 'la nostalgie de la boue'—a yearning for filth—and who are we in this day and age with our permissive society that turns a blind eye on 'porn-shops' and nude shows and obscene paperbacks, to bat an eye-lid?

With regard to style in drawing, Rowlandson hardly changed in the course of his long career. What Blake called 'the bounding line and its infinite inflections and movements' had one of its greatest practitioners in Rowlandson. He used a reed pen, sharpened to a fine point. He seldom used shading but suggested volume with free-flowing lines of loops and curves. His drawings are easily recognizable because of this idiosyncratic method. Perspective he sometimes altered, too, in order to accommodate a crowd in a street, or a large group in a room; his *Assembly Room, Bath*, has figures out of proportion and per-spective with the architectural background.

His drawings of rural England must not be ignored, however, nor his animal sketches, which are accurate and well-observed. Among his book illustrations are those for *The Microcosm of London* and the *Miseries of Human Life* (1808) and his popular *Tours of Dr. Syntax*, which depicts the miseries of the traveller on the road. Syntax on his bony nag may remind us of Don Quixote, but was meant as a good-natured satire of the wandering artist in search of the 'picturesque'. The adventures of Dr. Syntax became such a popular best-seller, when issued later as a separate book, that there soon followed Syntax hats, wigs and coats in the shops—a forerunner of our own Beatles craze! This book was followed by *Dr. Syntax in Search of Consolation* and *Dr. Syntax in Search of a Wife*, again with cartoons by Rowland-son, all as lively as ever (Plate 2).

The revival of colour-printing by the use of wood-blocks in the mid-nineteenth century by Edmund Evans brought a new race of

artist illustrators into being; the books gave them an assured liveli-
hood and the public responded by buying these delightful children's stories, which became recognized as the best in the world.
Kate Greenaway (1846–1901), Randolph Caldecott (1846–1886)
and Walter Crane (1845–1915) were among the foremost. Their
books continue to delight children the world over, and the
original drawings made for them are much treasured. Their
tasteful colour and decorative line make them works of art.

The invention of new colour-reproduction processes at the end
of the century gave artists greater scope in their illustrations and
Edmund Dulac (1882–1953), Arthur Rackham (1867–1939) and
Sir William Russell Flint (still living) made paintings of a rich
and sensuous colour. Beatrix Potter (1866–1946) used her inti-
mate knowledge of the wee beasties of the hedgerow to illustrate
her stories; they appealed to children because her own outlook
was childlike and naïve with a pure vein of poetic truth.

Among cartoonists must be mentioned Charles Keene (1823–
1891), regarded by many[1] as the greatest draughtsman of the
nineteenth century. His pen and ink drawings are lively in line,
with sometimes malicious comments on the foibles of society.
We may think the captions overlong and the jokes rather tame
these days, but there is no denying their power as works of art in
their own right. He observed carefully and recorded the gestures, dress and mannerisms of his day.

The prices of these drawings in the salerooms vary from a few
pounds (pencil or rough crayon sketches) to a few hundreds for
completely worked out drawings in colour. The prices of the
illustrators are rapidly rising; if you are wise, you will buy any
you come across quickly; but beware of copies and imitations done
by amateur hands.

[1] Walter Sickert was one. Martin Hardie in *The Victorians* allows Keene's
greatness as a draughtsman, but denies him a high place as a watercolour artist.

8. The Twentieth Century

IT is difficult to assess the art of one's own times, and the best I can do is give some guidance to the collector about the main trends and movements of the past sixty years, indicating some of the outstanding figures. The artists of Britain, will, of course, be mentioned, but a few continental artists who settled here cannot be left out, as their works come up for sale from time to time and are valuable contributions to our culture.

The art of the twentieth century has been said to start with Whistler, who was a rebel against the 'anecdotal' works that were fashionable at the turn of the century, works which 'relied on the intrinsic pathos or humour of their subjects rather than upon their own power of representing them with originality and insight; they still saw in terms of outline, when the leaders of European art were perfecting the new language of tone.'[1]

Whistler advocated and practised in his works a break with the academic tradition. Influenced by Japanese art, he used an economic and expressive design, avoiding mythology and history and looking to the world around him; the Impressionists gave him a sense of atmosphere, Corot, Hals and Rembrandt a sense of tone. 'Nature contains the elements,' he wrote, 'as the keyboard contains the notes of music.' and he goes on to elaborate this metaphor, suggesting that the artist must then manipulate these 'notes' to make his own pattern or 'music' on the canvas. His *Nocturnes* are aptly named; they were paint-notes made into a pattern, rather than literal transcripts of nature. An abstract quality of line and tone, apart from any social purpose, is invoked, and his influence on English painting of this century is and was very great.

[1] *An Introduction to English Painting*, John Rothenstein.

Other influences were at work, too; the accessibility of foreign works, ease of travel, photography and improved colour-printing methods put within reach of artists and public alike the works of all schools of painting from all over the world. It is difficult to see a main stream with all the 'schools' and influences affecting the artist.

Continental painting already made artists aware of the Impressionists' plea for the play of bright, prismatic colours; the native tradition of realism and the attractions of abstract art were present, too. A school of London Impressionists came into existence with Walter Richard Sickert (1860–1942) and Philip Wilson Steer (1860–1942) who practised *plein air* painting, which was not much favoured by the former, who preferred to work in the studio after collecting notes and impressions of the scene. Wilson Steer's watercolours are clean and sparkling with a fresh-air spontaneity about them that is very near to the affectionate renderings of Constable. Tom Collier was a master whose skies are full of light and shining clouds.

Pissarro, Ethel Walker, Tonks and McEvoy, J. D. Innes and Gwen John followed in the tradition, producing drawings and watercolours of the same freshness and sensitiveness. During the short span of his life J. D. Innes (1887–1914) made a number of drawings of his native Wales and in France (Plate 32), which are masterly and economic evocations of the scene. Augustus John is powerful in his portraits, but his sister Gwen achieved a subtlety and intensity far beyond him. Her drawings are much prized today and have a lasting depth and charm. Her *Young Man Sketching* (Plate 36) is in my collection.

The New English Art Club in the first decades of the century included Spencer Gore (1878–1914), Harold Gilman (1876–1919) and Charles Ginner (1878–1952); their paintings and drawings were pre-occupied with the post-impressionist sense of design and construction. Cubist influence shows in Gore's work. Ginner advocated a 'Neo-realism' and held up Van Gogh as its most intense exponent.

A new influence, that of 'vorticism' came into the art scene with the work of Percy Wyndham Lewis (1882–1957). He absorbed the tenets of the Futurists, who tried to paint the 'vortex of modern life—a life of steel, fever, pride and headlong speed'. Lewis revived again Whistler's plea for a visual language as abstract as music. This striving after a semi-abstract pattern, based on the elements of reality that the artist chooses, shows in his landscapes and portraits.

William Roberts (b. 1895) and Edward Wadsworth (1889–1949) carried on the vorticist and cubist methods, each evolving later a highly personal style: Roberts made his figures in a semi-abstracted form like tubular pieces of machinery, while Wadsworth juxtaposed incongruous objects in his landscapes much in the manner of the surrealists. Their drawings in pen and ink and their watercolours are vigorously conceived and novel in approach. Edward Burra (b. 1905) and Tristram Hillier (b. 1905), take the surrealist element a stage further. Sexual symbolism and fantasy combine to give a macabre note, not altogether pleasing but exciting and searching to a degree, as they explore the deeper recesses of the mind with a probing pencil that is almost a scalpel.

The First World War made a halt in these exciting movements, but also brought into prominence and matured a new race of artists, who visited the battle-fields and recorded their impressions. Paul Nash (1889–1946) saw landscapes as 'personalities'; French realism gave him the symbolic forms seen later in so many of his drawings, which bear an intensely personal vision of the world (Plate 34). C. R. W. Nevinson (1889–1946) was another official war-artist, strongly influenced by the Futurists.

Apart from these by nature and inspiration stood Stanley Spencer (1891–1959) who went on with his visionary renderings of Bible scenes, using his native Cookham for the characters and backgrounds. The influence of Italian primitives shows in the purity of line and the simplified tones he used. His drawings, preliminary sketches from life, are idiosyncratic records of figure and landscape, where the later semi-abstracted pattern can be seen. His pencil drawings are fairly modest in price and may be bought for under £40.

Matthew Smith (1879–1959) is more voluptuous in colour. He

attended as a young man a school run by Matisse, and his early
paintings are in the 'Fauve' manner of bright and often crude
colour.   His watercolours show the same richness of colour.

Abstract art is shown in the works of Ben Nicolson (b. 1894),
who often used raised surfaces by adhering layers of canvas or
thin wood to the foundation canvas.   Gouache, ink and watercolour appear in his pictures, combined with an elegant, fastidious
taste for line and tone.   Another abstract artist, who early in his
career as a member of the Euston Road Group had painted realistic
pictures, was Victor Pasmore.   Claude Rogers and Graham Bell
were also members of the group, who shared with Sickert an
enthusiasm for the post-impressionist style of painting. Francis
Hodgkin (1809–1947) was another member, who had a very
personal way of treating still-life and landscape in a formalized,
decorative way that shows the influence of Matisse.

Other artists of the modern school were Christopher Wood
(1901–1930) who painted landscapes and figures in a lyrical,
almost naïve style; Ivon Hitchens (b. 1893) used a sweeping
brush-stroke that tends towards abstraction in his landscapes of
the woodlands round his home in Sussex.   David Jones (b. 1895)
uses pencil and pen in flowing lines, combined with delicate
nuances of colour to illustrate Celtic legends; even his landscapes
and figure studies in the illustrations of his own war reminiscences
In Parenthesis have a lyrical line and a deeply personal sense of
pattern that expresses his religious beliefs.   They remind me of
the ancient Celtic interlacing patterns, and many historians see
in these, too, a mystical affirmation of faith in the poetic life of
man and the universe.   J. D. Innes (1884–1914) produced many
drawings of a singular beauty and economy of line.

Deeply felt are the watercolours of Edward Bawden (b. 1903).
Trained as a designer, he introduced into his drawings a wide
range of technical devices to create surface textures of an in-
genious intricacy.

More down to earth is L. S. Lowry (b. 1887), whose pen and
pencil studies of industrial scenes and characters of his native
Lancashire are still obtainable for £100 or less.   Ceri Richards
(b. 1903) is more exuberant, almost surrealist (Plate 33).   His

19. J. M. W. Turner: *St. Agatha's Abbey, Easby, Yorkshire, from the River Swale*; watercolour, gouache, and surface scratching. *Whitworth Art Gallery, Manchester*

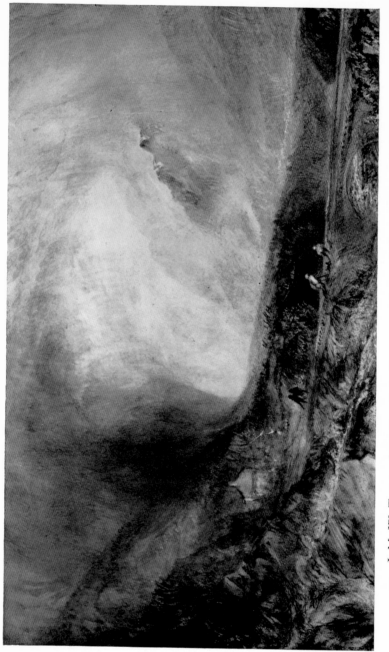

20. J. M. W. Turner: *Storm in a Swiss Pass*; watercolour. *Whitworth Art Gallery, Manchester*

21. Sir James Thornhill: *A Group of the Gods;* ink and brown washes. Lugt: Sir Bruce Ingram. *Author's collection*

22. Sir G. Kneller: *Venus and Adonis*; pen and brown ink and watercolour. Lugt: Sir Bruce Ingram. *Author's collection*

23.   Benjamin West: *Britannia surrounded by Symbolic Figures*; pen and
black ink.   *Author's collection*

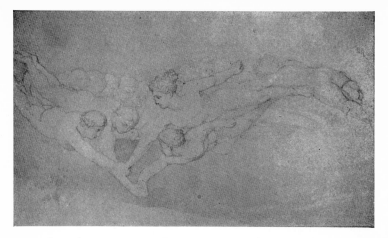

24. John Flaxman: *Descending Spirits*; pencil and wash. *Author's collection*

25. J. H. Mortimer: *Hercules and Antaeus*; pen and grey ink and grey washes. *Author's collection*

26. Sir Edward Burne-Jones: *Phyllis and Demophoön; Study;* crayon, watercolour and gouache. *By permission of the National Museum of Wales*

27. Dante Gabriel Rossetti: *David as King*; drawing. *By permission of the National Museum of Wales*

28. Sir L. Alma-Tadema: *Day-Dreams*; watercolour. *Author's collection*

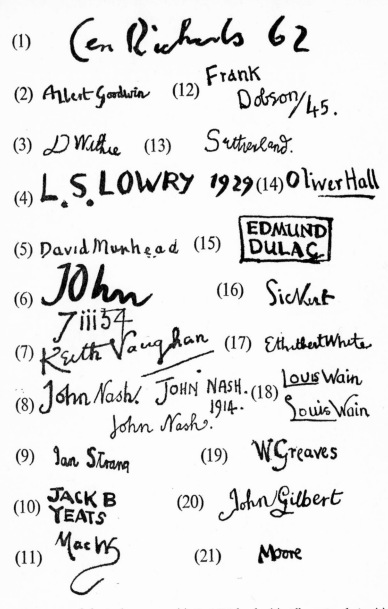

(1) Ceri Richards 62

(2) Albert Goodwin   (12) Frank Dobson/45.

(3) D Wilkie   (13) Sutherland.

(4) L. S. LOWRY 1929 (14) Oliver Hall

(5) David Muirhead   (15) EDMUND DULAC

(6) JOhn   (16) Sickert

(7) 7 iii 54 Keith Vaughan   (17) Ethelbert White

(8) John Nash/ JOHN NASH. 1914. John Nash.   (18) Louis Wain / Louis Wain

(9) Ian Strang   (19) W Greaves

(10) JACK B YEATS   (20) John Gilbert

(11) Mac W   (21) Moore

Signatures of the 20th century, (1) Ceri Richards, (2) Albert Goodwin, (3) David Wilkie, (4) L. S. Lowry, (5) David Muirhead, (6) Augustus John, (7) Keith Vaughan, (8) John Nash, (9) Ian Strang, (10) Jack B. Yeats, (11) J. Mac-Whirter, (12) Frank Dobson, (13) Graham Sutherland, (14) Oliver Hall, (15) Edmund Dulac, (16) W. R. Sickert, (17) Ethelbert White, (18) Louis Wain, (19) W. Greaves, (20) John Gilbert, (21) Henry Moore

illustrations of LA CATHEDRALE ENGLOUTIE and the poems of Dylan Thomas are rich in colour and line and his drawings in ink, gouache and watercolour may be bought for about £100, his smaller studies for less.

Among other artists of the present day may be mentioned David Hockney, whose figure studies in pen and pencil are affectionately observed (if you like male nudes!); Leslie Worth's watercolour landscapes and illustrations; Henry Liverton's restrained washes to suggest wide reaches of river and shore, and Sir William Russell Flint's wet-washed Spanish landscapes and village scenes, embellished with curvacious beauties, often nude. Their prices range from £100 to £400 and are well worth the investment.

The illustrators and cartoonists must not be forgotten, for their work gives a lasting record of the scene. The drawings of Giles, Phil May, 'Vicky' and Heath Robinson may be bought for twenty or thirty pounds, and may very well appreciate in value in a few years' time; Laura Knight specialized in circus and ballet scenes; Lucy Kemp-Welch in cattle and horses; W. Heath Robinson's Arabian Nights illustrations, not to mention his political and social squibs; Louis Wain's cat-portraits, both whimsical and horrific; Sir Alfred Munnings's horses and stable hands as well as the aristocratic ladies and gentlemen owners; these are only a few of the treasures still to be had for two figures. Peter Scott, A. Thorburn and Tunnicliffe show their affection for wild life, too, and Mildred Eldridge records the butterflies, birds and bees with affectionate detail. E. H. Shepard (of 'Pooh' fame) has also produced numerous drawings of great sensitivity and charm.

The preliminary drawings done for book-illustrations by Kate Greenaway, Beatrix Potter, Walter Crane and R. Caldecott and A. Rackham are also to be seen in the salerooms; their prices are soaring, so buy them quickly!

9. Monograms and Signatures

TURNER once remarked, upon being asked about his missing signature on a painting that it was 'signed all over'. And that is true of the works of great artists. No one can mistake a painting by Constable, Gainsborough, Girtin or Cotman for anything else; their style, indicative of a rich and strong personality and command of technical skill, is written all over the drawing. Even if their works were not signed (and many are not) there could be no doubt about their authenticity to the practised eye.

It is the lesser artists who are the problems, especially as so many of them show the influence of the greater ones who were often their teachers, or whose work they copied or imitated to make a sale. I have already alluded to the work of John Varley, who imitated Wilson and Claude; other artists like Brabazon imitated Turner in his free-flowing, highly-coloured gouaches, and numerous were the imitators of David Cox—even his signature is forged on some of his drawings. The collector would be wise to cast a dubious eye on any drawing which looks clumsy in execution or crude in colour, if it bears the signature of a great artist.

It must be remembered, however, that many artists hardly ever signed their works. Charles Davidson produced many Sussex landscapes which are charming and competently done. Few have his signature. I like his work, although they are not highly praised by the critics and may be bought for a few pounds in the salerooms. The detailed painting of the trees and the gradations of tone to suggest distances are as unaffected as Crome's and almost as good. His colour scheme of muted greens and blues and golds is his signature.

Monograms and Initials, (1) James Ward, (2) William Blake, (3) William Marlowe, (4) Ford Madox Brown, (5) Aubrey Beardsley, (6) D. G. Rossetti, (7) T. M. Richardson, (8) Eleanor F. Brickdale, (9) Simeon Solomon, (10) C. Pissarro, (11) Pierre Bonnard, (12) E. J. Millais, (13) Frank Brangwyn, (14) Charles Ricketts, (15) Birket Foster, (16) E. M. Wimperis, (17) Eric Gill, (18) George Vincent, (19) John Middleton, (20) J. M. Whistler

Another artist whose work is seldom seen in the salerooms is Jock Wilson, a Devonshire man. His drawings have a delicate colour-pattern of turquoise and gold, and the surface is mottled in a most peculiar way—perhaps by the use of a size mixture or a glaze in the final wash (he was, I think, a scene-painter)[1]—and are quite an innovation. Many of his drawings are unsigned, but may be recognized by this technique.

Some artists used a monogram: Birket-Foster comes to mind. Many of his landscapes and pencil-sketches bear this monogram, which is often alluded to as a 'studio-stamp'. Whistler invented the 'butterfly' motif from the initials of his name; Charles Ricketts and Aubrey Beardsley used their initials as well as their full names; Millais, too, often signed with a monogram, reproduced in my drawing. Frank Brangwyn, E. M. Wimperis and Mac Whirter often used their initials. In earlier times, William Blake wrote a florid 'W. B.' and Fuseli a scribbled 'H. F.' which the experienced will recognize; other artists used their surnames only. Copley-Fielding is an example and Clarkson Stanfield too. Some artists inscribed the name of the place they painted, Thomas Bush-Hardy often inscribed his paintings with a note of the scene, 'The Harbour Bar—T. B. Hardy—1890', and Constable also added detailed descriptions on the verso as well as making a note of time of day and any atmospheric effects he had no time to record. The writing of these men must be remembered, and may give a valuable clue to the authorship of a drawing, if there is any doubt. The astute collector becomes an expert in calligraphy in the end, looking at the back of the drawing (the 'verso' they call it in the trade) for any clues such as date, place, and any other comments by the artist.

I have reproduced a few of these monograms and signatures for the guidance of beginners on the delicate and tortuous paths of collecting; but it should be remembered that an artist's signature may vary with age and health. The three signatures of John Nash are all genuine; they show the change in the artist's calli-

---

[1] Some one may write a monograph one day on the scene-painters who became landscape artists: Cox, Barrett, Jock Wilson, Sam Bough and Clarkson Stanfield.

graphy over a span of twenty or thirty years, so a signature which looks very different from another by the same artist should not be dismissed as a forgery: a man's writing, like his painting, changes a little over the years.

Other things must be borne in mind, too. A drawing of the eighteenth century or earlier must be on a paper of that period. Large sheets were unobtainable, as also was a paper of a pure white like the modern painting paper. A water-mark often shows or a series of parallel lines recording the pressing process. Thick card was used by many artists and this may have a semi-absorbent surface which is almost hairy in texture; it is often mottled and uneven in colour; the 'oatmeal' paper of David Cox's latter years comes to mind and the pale mushroom-coloured paper of so many of Morland's drawings; they are not discoloured by age; this was their natural colour.

Another guide is the colour of the ink. Early drawings seldom have ink of a deep and pure black; slight fading to brown or grey is almost always apparent, and a reed pen will show slight blobs and scratches in the lines which are characteristic of this kind of drawing not seen in a modern steel nib. All these clues, as well as the style, are a good guide to the age, authorship and provenance.

(1) J T Serres fect   (11) R. Dadd

(2) W. L. Leitch   (12) J Crome.

(3) T. L. Rowbotham Jun i 1850   (13) M E Cotman

(4) Strasbourg S. Prout. (14) J Sillett

(5) Sowden   (15) H Bright

(6) E. Lander   (16) Cotman

(7) John Wheatley   (17) Sam Alken

(8) Henry Jutsum   (18) G. Morland 1792.

(9) Charles Dixon.   (19) S. Gilpin.

(10) C T Dixon   (20) S Howitt.

Signatures of: (1) J. T. Serres, (2) W. L. Leitch, (3) T. L. Rowbotham Jun., (4) Samuel Prout, (5) J. Sowden, (6) E. Lander, (7) J. Wheatley, (8) H. Jutsum, (9) C. Dixon, (10) C. T. Dixon, (11) Richard Dadd, (12) John ('OLD) Crome, (13) M. E. Cotman, (14) J. Sillett, (15) Henry Bright, (16) J. S. Cotman, (17) S. Alken, (18) George Morland, (19) Sawrey Gilpin, (10) Samuel Howitt

(1) *S Palmer*

(2) *S D Colkett*

(3) *Jon: Constable f 1812*

(4) *J Varly*

(5) *Alexr Cozens*

(6) *G M Moser*

(7) *Fuseli P.T*

(8) *W. Payne*

(9) *Girtin*

(10) *Cipriani*

(11) *F Towne*

(12) *S. H. Grimm*

(13) *John Cozens*

(14) *F Swaine*

(15) *Mortimer*

(16) *J. Rowlandson*

(17) *O Humphry*

(18) *AUBREY BEARDSLEY.*

(19) *David Cox*

(20) *W R Beverley*

(21) *Edward Lear*

(22) *J. Sturgess.*

Signatures of: (1) Samuel Palmer, (2) S. D. Colkett, (3) John Constable, (4) John Varley, (5) A. Cozens, (6) G. M. Moser, (7) H. Fuseli, (8) W. Payne, (9) T. Girtin, (10) G. B. Cipriani, (11) F. Towne, (12) S. H. Grimm, (13) J. R. Cozens, (14) F. Swaine, (15) J. H. Mortimer, (16) T. Rowlandson, (17) O. Humphry, (18) Aubrey Beardsley, (19) David Cox, (20) W. R. Beverley, (21) Edward Lear, (22) John Sturgess

10. The Saleroom: Viewing and Bidding

EQUIPPED at last for the hazards of buying, the collector proceeds to the saleroom; but the wise buyer always *inspects* the goods offered for sale.

And this is even more essential when purchasing drawings and paintings; an astute eye can gather a good deal of information from a careful examination of the works, which can be seen at least two days before the sale. There is ample time to look at the pictures and drawings and to examine the parcels 'in folio'. These are unframed—often unmounted—drawings, which are held between a large folded sheet of stiff white paper, bearing on the outside in large letters an indication of the number of the lot and how many drawings are included. Thus 'LOT 7/ 6' means that the item is number 7 in the catalogue and six drawings are included. There may be any number of drawings in the same lot; and as only one or two of these will be shown when the bidding is in progress, the wise collector would do well to examine them all. There may be some treasure lurking among the others. (I recently picked up a very lovely drawing by Alma-Tadema, which was included in such a parcel, though this was not shown during the sale, and I believe accounted for the low price of the lot.) So examine all drawings carefully, asking yourself: is it a genuine work in the artist's usual style of drawing and colouring? Is the signature or monogram his? Is there any inscription at the back? Is the ink used in the drawing of the same tone and colour as the writing? If not, then it may be an interpolation by a later hand. Is there a price-tag on the back of the mount, or details of a previous sale, or a collector's mark? (The well-known collectors may be relied upon to acquire only good and genuine works). The sales label may be that of the home-town of the artist or in the same locality; it may be regarded as fairly genuine in this case and a good guide as to authenticity.

I mentioned the mount, and this is also a sound method of assessing age. A gold mount indicates that the painting was executed before 1905 at least, when gold mounts began to go out of fashion. A narrow strip of gold followed this fashion and finally white mounts or cream. French artists liked blue mounts. Pale brown is seen in the Netherlands. Modern artists often have a preference for mounts of a deep tint of red or blue, especially for pen and ink drawings. A drawing cut out and 'laid' on card with an inked-in rectangle all round is often a sign of a late-nineteenth century artist's work. Many of the works by Varley, Sandby and Dayes are mounted in this way, though a deeply cut modern mount may be added by a later framer for effect.

The frame may yield some information, too. Look at the back for labels again; is the maker indicated? (The address will give you valuable clues as to date.) Is the frame a carved wood one or wood embellished with gesso or plaster? (Some dealers insert a fine needle into the frame: if it is wood the needle goes in a little way; if it is plaster, it does not!) Needless to say, the carved wood frame adds to the value of the picture. You cannot, of course, examine the drawing in detail, if it is glazed and framed; but you may be lucky, when you take it home and look inside. I heard of one buyer who found six David Cox drawings inside: subsequent drawings had been laid on the same stretcher by the artist. But this kind of good fortune is not likely to come your way in the larger salerooms. The assistants almost always take the drawings out of the frames to examine them and will separate them if there are a number inside. A country sale is another matter; the auctioneer and his busy assistants have not the time or the flair for such work, and you may be lucky.[1]

Be careful, too, about attribution in the catalogues. This is not always accurate. I once bought a drawing in a reputable London saleroom, labelled 'Cipriani', which later turned out to be a Dutch drawing. I mentioned this to the sales clerk later,

[1] I once found a charming watercolour used as a backing for a portrait.

and he laughingly remarked: 'Oh, so long as we put something in the catalogue, everybody's happy. If we're not sure, we put *something* down.' There is a dreadful warning somewhere in that pronouncement. On the whole, however, the attributions are painstaking and the result of careful thought on the part of the experts. The new law that safeguards the interests of the buyer at sales must also be borne in mind: it is now an offence to pronounce a work genuine or attribute it to a certain artist if this is found to be incorrect. The saleroom and the auctioneer safeguard themselves by setting forth at the beginning of the catalogue the 'conditions of Sale'; and the beginner should read these conditions carefully.

He should also understand the 'code' by which all catalogues are prepared. Briefly, it is as follows: if a drawing is labelled in the catalogue as 'Gainsborough', then it is 'a work of the school or by one of the followers of the artist or in his style and of uncertain date.' If the work is preceded by the surname and initials— 'T. Gainsborough', then it is 'a work of the period of the artist, which may be wholly or in part his work.' But if it has the christian or forename(s) of the artist and the surname, followed by his decorations, then it is 'in our opinion a work by the artist'. So the description 'Thomas Gainsborough, R. A.' expresses an opinion of the genuineness of the painting or drawing offered for sale. 'Signed' means that it has a recognized signature of the artist. 'Bears signature' however, means that this 'may be the signature of the artist'. The term 'dated' in the catalogue means that the work was executed at that date; but 'bears date' means that the work *may* have been executed at that time. The buyer is protected too by the following clause: 'If within 21 days after the sale the buyer of any lot returns the same and proves that considered in the light of the catalogue entry the lot is a deliberate forgery then the sale of the lot will be rescinded and the purchase price of the same refunded.'

If you study carefully the above, you will soon be conversant with the catalogue 'code'. Larger salerooms are run on perfectly honest and straightforward lines, and I have never come across the 'rings' which have been so much in the news since the

Duccio affair. One is aware of the dealers, of course; one cannot help hearing their names and seeing the familiar faces time and again. Country sales are much more chancy in procedure and method. Watercolours may be labelled as 'paintings' or prints, even as etchings, and colour-prints described as 'drawings'. So one must be on guard. Dirty glass and ancient varnish are also misleading; while 'parcels' or the job lots at the end may include genuine drawings, photographs and even samplers. In the hugger-mugger of furniture and household goods, which have to be disposed of in a day, pictures often get short shrift indeed. So keep your eyes open: you may get a bargain.

Beware of the colour-prints. From a distance they may look like genuine drawings. There is no thickness of paint, as in an oil-painting to help the casual observer; but if you turn the drawing slightly sideways you will soon learn to recognize the unevenness of the paint surface; glycerine gives a varying intensity and 'shine' to different colours (intense colours like Prussian blue and crimson often show this); while scraping out or washing out will give textures which are quite impossible in a print. The use of body-colour or gouache can also be seen with the naked eye: there is a certain thickness to the blobs of paint which show a raised edge; and if the gouache technique is used throughout, as in many of W. H. Hunt's paintings, it gives a pearly or milky smoothness to the colours not obtainable in any other way and certainly not to be seen in the print. If you can touch the paper discreetly, then you can test its surface textures; a painting has a slight roughness here and there; it smells differently, too. The older the paper, the more musty its smell will be. Old size, glycerine—or honey, barley-sugar, porter, beer or gin—leave a slight aroma which no print ever had or will have. Printing-ink has its own, unmistakable smell, which is not that of paint. Pencil marks or pen and ink work, if examined through a magnifying glass, also reveal variations; they may dent the paper slightly or leave fuzzy, broken edges and flicks, showing the artist's nervous excitement with his subject.

Drawings often bear some mark on the mount or on the back, indicating the name of the collector; there may be a written note as well.   If the drawing comes from a famous collector, then you may be sure that it is a good one, and the catalogue will give a detailed history of its provenance.   There may be a photograph, too.   The more information the catalogue provides about the drawing and its previous owners, whether it has been used to illustrate any literature about the artist (biographies or articles in Art journals), then you may be sure that the drawing will fetch a very high price.

A Dutch scholar and collector by the name of Fritz Lugt made a scientific study of collectors' marks, which he published in two large volumes.   Such references are now known by his name, that is, the term 'Lugt' in a catalogue refers to the collector's mark or inscriptions on the drawing and to its known history.   The mark may be the intials or some heraldic sign or family crest or an embossed stamp.   These are on the back or the mount and do not damage the drawing in any way.

One of the earliest collectors in Britain was Sir Peter Lely, who stamped the drawings in his collection with 'P. L.' 'P. H. L.' is sometimes found on them.   These are the initials of Prosper Henry Lankrink, a pupil of Lely, who bought many of his master's drawings at the sale after his death.   Artists very often collected drawings to study, and often to imitate.   Sir Joshua Reynolds, Richard Cosway and Jonathan Richardson and his son may be mentioned.   Paul Sandby and Benjamin West, too, collected drawings.   In the days before our great national galleries came into existence, this was the only way to study the works of the masters, and many noblemen employed artists to make copies of great paintings in Italy and the Netherlands; the human cameras served a very useful and aesthetic purpose.   These copies could then be displayed to guests and visiting artists.   Many original drawings were also acquired on the Grand Tour; they were comparatively cheap then.   Today you would have to spend many hundreds—perhaps thousands of pounds—to buy a drawing by Raphael or Rembrandt.   They were not highly prized in the old days, but were eagerly sought after by private collectors.

These drawings may be beyond the reach of the modest collector, but pencil, pen and ink or charcoal sketches by such artists as Benjamin West, Romney, Lawrence and Reynolds may be bought for two figures. Parcels often contain examples of their work. They may not be finished works of art, but they provide vital glimpses of the mind and hand of the great masters. Late nineteenth-century artists such as Alma-Tadema, Burne-Jones, Rossetti and Holman Hunt made a great many studies from life, still-life and architecture as preliminary drawings for their paintings; and these are well worth the thirty or forty pounds they fetch in the sale-rooms.

You should, of course, make a note in your catalogue of any particular lot which you fancy. In parcels especially, it is almost impossible to remember in detail what the different items are. The description in the catalogue may just say 'drawings by or attributed to D. Cox, J. Varley, Nibbs and Rossetti', and there may be one or two by these artists or many more. If you are wise you will scribble a note about the drawings, because only one or two will be held up by the assistant when the parcel is shown for sale. And you may lose the drawing you liked!

All lots are displayed at the sale. And please get there promptly. Christie's sales usually commence at eleven in the morning, unless otherwise stated; Sotheby's sales of drawings and watercolours in the afternoon at 2.30. Tuesdays and Thursdays are the chosen days, the sales being spaced out like this to accommodate buyers who travel specially to London to attend them. Other salerooms such as Harrods, Bonhams and Knight, Frank and Rutley usually avoid these times and try to fit in their sales on other days. Announcements of the dates and times appear in the *Sunday Times*, every fortnight; *The Times* on Tuesdays, the *Daily Telegraph* on Mondays and in such magazines as *Arts Review*, *Apollo* and the *Connoisseur*. Subscription for catalogues for all sales of drawings and the price-lists is about four guineas per annum and is a sound investment for the collector. I always mark my catalogues with the details of previous prices, if I cannot attend the sales personally. The prices are a good guide for future purchases, though the quality of a work will often send the price soaring, if it is by a sought-after artist whose works are scarce. A glance at sales trends is sometimes advisable: if you are buying for investment, buy the works of the artist whose prices appear to be rising. The big names, however, will always be a sound invest-ment; and most artists' works show a gradual rise over recent years.[1]

Arrived at the saleroom, you will find a number of chairs arranged to face the auctioneer's desk. Tables for the sales clerks and assistants are at the side. The lots are stacked at the back, brought forward and held up to view by the porters, and are usually sold in the order in which they appear in the catalogue. If any lot is withdrawn it is announced by the auctioneer during the sale. Notices are put up too, on the wall, where the lots are displayed, so look out for these to avoid disappointment, if you have taken a particular fancy to some drawing. Do not forget, too, that there may be a 'reserve price' on a drawing or painting, and the auctioneer may put down a work if this reserve price is not reached, or one of his assistants may bid until the reserve price is reached.

When the sale is on, the assistants or porters show the pictures, sometimes propping them up on easels, sometimes walking up and down in the aisle between the chairs. If you want to examine a work closely, they will oblige by stopping for a moment, but you must make up your mind quickly, as the bidding is still going on.

Bidding usually starts at two pounds. If there is no response, the auctioneer may reduce it to a pound; if there is still no response, he will say 'Pass' and the lot is put down and the next one is put up. Bids go up by a pound to ten pounds, then by two to twenty, then by fives, and so on. After reaching the hundred, the bids may rise by twenty or more. After a thousand by five hundred. If a high sum is expected for a drawing, or if a bid has been received in writing, the bidding may start at this figure.

When the last bid has been called, and this seems to be the final one, the auctioneer will bring down his hammer, and the lot is yours. If there is an objection—I once heard a lady call out that she was still bidding—the lot is put up again and the bidding goes on. You have to be smart and bid by calling out

[1] A recent survey of art sales, published in *The Times* Saturday Review, showed an increase of thirteen times in the price of watercolours since 1951.

or by raising your hand or catalogue or nodding. Saleroom etiquette requires that you do not turn round and look at the other bidders.

If this is your first purchase, the sales clerk or one of his assistants will present you with a slip for signature and this you will keep until the end of the sale, when you are expected to pay and, if possible, to collect your purchase. After a while, they get to know you and will remember your name and face. They will then keep your slip until the end.

It is then that you collect your pictures by presenting yourself, your slip and your cheque at the desk of the sales clerk. The slip is in two parts; once it has been receipted, you will be given one half to keep, and this you will show to the assistants at the back, who will then give you your purchases. For a small tip—about half-a-crown or five shillings is the usual—they will wrap up your pictures for you in brown paper; though not so long ago there was no effort to do this and one could see portly gentlemen and elderly ladies walking along New Bond Street with pictures tucked under their arms. I used to take with me a ball of string and some wrapping paper. I got curious looks, but they got the message, and the paper and string appeared soon afterwards!

Any drawings and paintings left are stored away safely for collection later. Sotheby's are not over fussy about the time limit, but other salerooms such as Christie's keep the pictures only for five days. After this they are stored elsewhere, and they may charge you a fee for storage if they are left for a considerable time.

If you cannot attend sales, bids may be sent by post. Specially printed slips are provided, or you may write your bid in the form of a letter, indicating the number of the Lot or Lots and the limit of your bid. This will then be recorded by the sales clerk who will put in a bid on your behalf. If you bid up to £25 on Lot 16, then he will call out bids *up to this amount*; so if the lot goes for sixteen or eighteen or twenty pounds, then it will be yours, if one of these is the highest bid; if the bids exceed your limit of twenty-five, then you have lost it. If you keep a list of the current prices for the works of certain artists that you fancy, you will soon learn how much to bid—though there can be surprises, of

29.   Robert Hills: *Cows in a Meadow*; watercolour.   *Author's collection*

30.   S. Gilpin: *Horse in a Wooded Landscape*; pencil drawing.   *Author's collection*

31. Samuel Howitt: *Stag being attacked by Hounds*; pen and brown ink and watercolour. *Author's collection*

32. J. D. Innes: *Noyouls, near Rodez*; pen and ink and watercolour. *Author's collection*

33. Ceri Richards: *The Source*; pen and ink and watercolour. *By permission of the National Museum of Wales*

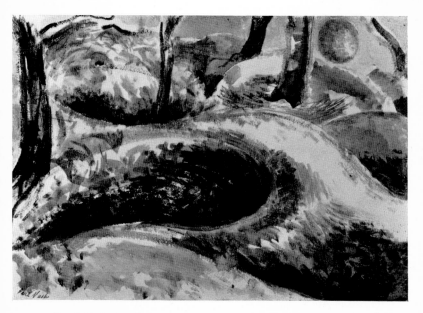

34. Paul Nash: *Landscape at Pen Pits*; watercolour. *Victoria & Albert Museum*

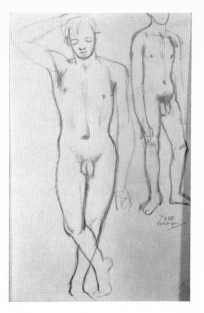

35. Keith Vaughan: *Figure Studies*; pencil.
Author's collection

36. Gwen John: *Young Man Sketching*; crayon.
Author's collection

course, in these days of rapidly rising prices, and an upper rather than a lower figure is the wiser course. It is no use being bitter after the sale and wishing you had bid more!

Remember, too that Christie's bid in guineas. I once lost a very nice painting by forgetting this rule. I bid 'up to £20',— the painting went for twenty guineas!

What prices should one pay for drawings? you may ask. And this is a question that arises early in the career of every collector. You may be able to afford only a few pounds a month; you may have a lucky win on the Pools and decide to go in for an expensive picture, or you may buy cautiously and begin in a small way. The latter is perhaps the wisest course, though every collector will eventually make up his own mind and go his own way. Every collection in the end, if it is a good one, will have a quality of its own. You may decide to collect the works of only one artist— and this can be a rewarding theme; or you may decide to collect drawings in crayon or charcoal, or only watercolours of sporting subjects, or figures—but whatever you decide to do, it is best to limit your choice to one field and be a specialist in a limited area rather than an indiscriminate collector of everything that comes your way. My next chapter deals with prices, and I have taken these over three years, to give you an idea of the changes in value and the fluctuation in the prices of the works of different artists.

I have shown the lowest, as well as the highest prices in my lists. These low prices are usually for pencil or charcoal sketches; but they are not to be despised, for they contain a good deal of excellent work. The highest prices are for finished paintings, that is, drawings completed with washes of watercolour and brought to a high standard of completion by the artist. Prices in brackets are those given for works where the attribution is rather doubtful; you must use your judgment about the value of these; personally, I like buying one or two occasionally; backing one's judgment is sometimes worth the risk of a few pounds. The fact that many of these 'dubious' drawings sometimes fetch quite high prices in the salerooms indicates that other collectors too, or those who run our art galleries and showrooms, feel that the drawings are indeed of great value and near enough to authenticated works as makes no difference. The individual collector must decide whether it is worth buying these 'dark horses'; they may not be out of the best stable; but on the other hand they may be after all worth the few pounds asked for them.

Incidentally do not expect to find salacious drawings in the salerooms. They will not handle erotic drawings, unless these are primitive works or sufficiently ancient—like Greek or Etruscan vases—to be 'respectable' antiques. There are, of course, a number of drawings in existence by artists like Fuseli and Rowlandson which often cross the border between art and pornography, but we should remember that such things were taken in their stride by the artists and public alike of those days. Nudes again are often sold; the female nude is openly displayed, however erotic the model may look in her undraped loveliness; the male nude is sometimes discreetly pushed into a dim corner or concealed 'in folio'. I once collected such a drawing and the porter very discreetly kept it face downwards on the table while he was wrapping it up for me! Such figure studies go relatively cheaply, especially those in charcoal or pencil and they are not to be despised, even if they look nothing more than a few hastily-drawn lines. They are often lively and informative and have the unmistakable stamp of the master's hand.

However slight, they are more than drawings; they are messages from majestic spirits of the past that can still give us the power to share that moment of communion with nature, enjoying again and again the solace of the tender and the beautiful.

11. Prices

'THERE is no such thing as a price', quotes Laurence Binyon in a final word to collectors.[1] But one has to think of prices when bidding and make up one's mind how much one can afford. It is an obvious truism that one buys to suit one's pocket, but one can also buy wisely and make a good speculation if one follows the trends in the art market.

Glancing at prices during the last few years, these trends appear fairly clearly: Samuel Palmer's drawings could be bought for about fifty pounds a few years ago; today you will be lucky to get one under a hundred! But his pencil sketches are still fairly cheap; one went for £20 in a recent sale. Another artist who has appreciated rapidly is Brabazon, an amateur who was not highly prized in his lifetime and who followed Turner in his use of bright gouache colours, suggestive of atmosphere and space.

But, speaking generally, all works of art have appreciated during the last few years. The indices and graphs published by *The Times* show this clearly: English paintings and drawings have appreciated about thirteen times since 1951 and are still on the upward trend. Old master drawings have gone up eighteen times. My own lists, compiled since 1965, show a sharp rise for some artists (the economic experts can work out averages, if they like: I prefer to leave the lists open to scrutiny and let each reader draw his own conclusions) and the speculator can work out his own graphs and indices and make a wise buy.

Robert Wraight in *The Art Game* devotes a chapter to this side of collecting and deduces what he describes as 'Laver's Law' as a recipe for quick returns: roughly speaking this is that the art of

[1] *English Watercolours*, Laurence Binyon.

one's grandfather's day will probably be the next in the popularity stakes and will soon command high prices on the market. French Impressionists paintings are now beyond the reach of the average buyer; the post-impressionists have gone the same way; then the Pre-Raphaelites and the anecdotal (once despised) Victorian artists now command high prices and have made a rapid comeback in popular esteem. Who will be next? I forecast the artists of the beginning of the century, or the twenties perhaps, so buy up all you can while the prices are at rock bottom; they are bound to go up soon.

12. Keeping Drawings Safely

IT was the custom among collectors in the eighteenth century to keep their drawings in large albums or portfolios and this method has much to recommend it. The drawings are safeguarded from fading, from dust and damp (if stored in a warm, dry place like a drawer or a bookcase in a living-room constantly heated) and the depredations of moth and other things that destroy paper, not to mention the rough handling of domestics and other careless people!

These albums sometimes come into the sale-rooms and it is remarkable how clean and fresh the drawings look. Not so the drawings one sees in frames. Many are so faded by constant exposure to sun and daylight that the blues have often disappeared. One can sometimes see the blue of the original under the mount. I have a James Bourne drawing which is quite golden in tone all over, but a quarter inch margin all round that was protected by the mount is still a fresh blue and green, as at first painted.

Modern saleroom technique is adept at protecting drawings, either in cellophane covers, which are admirable, or by wrapping them in 'folio', that is a large double sheet of thick white paper.

If drawings are framed, see that the back of the picture is adequately sealed and that there is a sheet of three-ply or hardboard firmly tacked or glued into place. If damp has affected the drawing and mould appears, this may be removed by careful drying. Spots of mould, formed by a fungus in the size, cannot be removed in any way.[1] They may disappear or lighten with time, but I know of no adequate remedy. On no account try to remove them with a sponge or brush: this will remove the

[1] They may, however, be neutralized with a bleaching agent such as H_2O_2, but this may also remove the paint.

paint, too.   Very dirty drawings can be cleaned by sponging them over *lightly*, or by applying a fine sable brush to the surface, but great care has to be exercised, in order not to remove the paint. The best thing I have found for cleaning grubby mounts and drawings is the crumbly centre of a slice of white bread; but great care must be exercised when rubbing this over the surface—or rolling the crumbs about with the palm of the hand—in order not to remove any delicate pencil-work or pale colours.   A crayon or charcoal drawing had better be left alone, or some essential and irreplaceable part of the drawing may be removed by the over-zealous 'restorer'.   Burne-Jones once affixed a note to the back of one of his watercolours to say that it was a watercolour drawing, not an oil-painting, as a warning about the danger of 'cleaning' that might result in the disappearance of the work entirely.

13. Index of Artists and Prices: 1966-68 in Salerooms

(Prices in brackets indicate that the atribution is doubtful.   Low prices are usually for pencil, pen and ink or crayon sketches.   The final column may be used by the collector to insert additional information that he may wish to record.)

	1966	*1967*	*1968*	
Abbey, E.			5	
Abbott, J. White,	300–630	50–350	65–90, 350	
Absolon, J.	2–5, 14–70	5–20, 105	15–40	
Ackermann, G.			89	
Adam, R.		3–5–32	28, 150–160	
Adamson, J. B.	25			
Adler, J.		31–55		
Ainsley, S. J.	3–4			
Alberti, G. V.	6		6	
Alderson, J. S.		5	15	
Aldin, C.	5–6	26	4–10–20	
Aldridge, F. J.			6	
Alexander, H.	5			
Alexander, W. M.	6–20, 50–300	70	10	
Alfred, W.		25		
Alice, H.R.H. Princess		9	10–18	
Alken, G.	(6)	15	(10)	
Alken, H. (Senior)	15, 75–130	20–60–120	(16)22–70	

	1966	*1967*	*1968*
Alken, H. (Junior)	15(16)	4–12	(20)50–70
Alken, S.	20–32	40	20
Allan, A.		5	
Allan, R. W.	5	8	22–40
Allingham, Helen	4–10–24		12–50–80
Allinson, A.		3	
Allom, T.	5–6, 14–32	6–18	33–40
Alma-Tadema, Laura	30		
Alma-Tadema, Sir L.	40	13–45	22–60
American School (nineteenth century)		20	
Anderson, R.			22
Anderson, W.	6–8, 50–75	8–75–90	(8)75–136
Andrews, G. H.	4–7	20	10
Andriessen, J.		35	
Annigoni, P.	10	16–35	16–45–57
Anning-Bell, R.	6		6
Anthonissen			120
Apol, L.			18–50
Applebee, J.		18	
Appleton, H.		18–32	
Ardizzone, E.	15–40	40	
Armfield, M.	5		
Armour, G. D.			3–8
Arundale, F.		15	52
Ashburnham, G. P.	6		
Asheton, W.	8		
Atkins, E. M.		6	

	1966	1967	1968
Barnard, H. W.	20		
Barnes, R.			16
Barrett, G. (Junior)	8–12–20, 30	12–30–42	12–45, 80
Barrett, G. (Senior)	20	15–40–225	35–68
Barron, H.			26–73
Barrow, J.			22
Barrow, W. D.			18
Barstow, M.			28
Bartlett, W. H.	4–22	18–32	75
Bartolozzi, F.			18–32, 146
Barton, Rose	3		12
Bateman, H. M.		3	6–18
Baumer, L.	5	16	2
Bawden, E.	42	20–60	8–30, 45
Bax, G. L.		42	
Bayes, W.	30		120
Baynes, F. J.		12	6
Baynes, J. M.	25–60	12	23
Beardsley, A.		850	300–1000
Bearne, E.	12	4	
Beaton, C.	6–18		12
Beaumont, A.		29	
Beaumont, Sir G.	18	4–23	6–20
Becker, E.	6–7	10	6–10
Beechey, Lady		11	
Beechey, Sir W.		17	12
Beer, J.			10, 140–420
Beerbohm, Sir M.	35–55, 100–180	230	10, 220–340
Belcher, G.	3		

	1966	1967	1968
Belleroche, W.	20		
Belleuse, P. C.		140	100
Belloc, H.		10	
Bennett, W.	18	10–32	10–32
Bentley, C.	12–15, 80	85	21–100
Bentley, N.			18
Berton, E.			20
Betts, J. W.		6	
Beverley, W. R.	7–25	3–14–30	2–50
Bewick, J.			10
Bewick, T.			50–280
Biddle, E. S.		10	10
Bigelow, Lady	35		
Bigelow, Larry			37
Birch, S. J. Lamorna	8–15	3–6	6, 20–38
Bird, Mary H.		10	
Birtles			8
Birtwhistle, C.	10		
Black, S.		20	
Blacklock, W. K.	20		
Blake, S.		20	
Blake, W.	75–100	120–220–700	
Blampeid, E.		18	
Bleuler, L.	11		
Bligh, J.			10
Blinks, T.		6	
Blomfield, R.			12
Boitard, L. P.	78		
Bolton, J.			25
Bomberg, D.			110–520

	1966	*1967*	*1968*
Bone, Sir M.	12	25–30	35
Bonheur, R.	12–18		
Bonington, R. P.	(10)168	9–260–854	(48)40–1000
Bosbom		2	
Bossoli, C.		22	
Bougereau, F.			8
Bough, S.	10–32	4–35	35–70–168
Boughton, G. H.	5–10		
Bourgeois, Sir P. F.		12	3
Bourne, Elizabeth	20		6
Bourne, J.	2–4–35	7–24–65	8–25–60
Bouvier, A.	15	7–14	10–12
Bouvier, J.			14
Bover, J.		3	
Boyd, A.	15		63–73
Boys, T. S.	(20)50–400	12–50–130, 820	35–100–820
Brabazon, H. B.	(6)10–60	16–42–65	(15)25–200– 550
Bradley, C.			12
Bradley, M.		2–10	
Bramley, V. W.	5		
Brandard, R.		42	42
Brandeis Antoinetta		25	44
Brangwyn, Sir F.	(3)10–70	6, 28–80	15–75
Branson, J.	24		
Bree, W. J.			28
Brett, J.		68	10
Brewer, H. C.			7–18
Brickdale, Eleanour F.	7–15		32–70

	1966	1967	1968
Bridell, F. L.		45	
Brierly, Sir O. W.		38	32–147
Briggs, H. B.		8–30	
Bright, Harry			30–42
Bright, Henry	5–10–70	8–28–73	18–55–420
Brill, R.			10
Briscoe, A.		4	10–16
Bristow, E.		30	
Britton, J.		16	
Brock, C. E.	10–20	40–220	
Brock, H. M.	15	30	
Brockhurst, G. L.			22
Brodzky, H.	3–10–12		6–10–25
Brookes, W.	3	9	48
Brown, F. Madox	45–78		
Brown, L. 'Capability'		48	48
Brown, S. T. M.			15
Browne, C. H.	8		
Browne, G.		3	3
Browne, H. K. ('Phizz')	2–18	7–8	4–35–70
Browne, T.	3–4	2	6–8–30
Brzeska, H. G.	25–90–210		157–230
Buck, A.	20	60	22
Buck, J.			15
Buck, S.		20	2–47
Buckler, J. C.	2–15	8	6–8, 14–30
Buckler, W.	12–15		
Buckley, C. F.			10–80
Bulwer, Rev. J.	18	6	6

	1966	*1967*	*1968*
Bunbury, H. W.	(1–17)34–60	6–22–70	9–22–38
Bundy, E.		45	25–42–47
Burgess, H. W.	4–10	10–16	1–9–70
Burgess, J. B.	20	8	100
Burgess, W. (of Dover)	14–50		25
Burn, R.			3
Burnard, Sir F. C.		3	
Burne-Jones, Sir E. C.	6–15, 40–170	14–25, 40–170, 850–1575	12–40, 70–850
Burnett, W. H.		5	
Burney, E. F.	40	22	20–55
Burr, J.			22
Burra, E.			315
Burt, A. R.			6
Burton, Sir F. W.		21	44
Bury, A.	5	8	3–8
Busk, Mary			10
Bussey, R.			8
Butler, Lady E.	5		
Butler, Mildred	2		7
Byrne, J.			65
Cadolini, G.			25
Caffieri, H.		40	15
Calcott, Sir A. W.			18
Calcott, W. J.	10	2–40	8–18
Caldecott, R.		8–22	8–12–22
Calder, A.			240
Callcott, Sir J. W.			10
Callender, A.	15	25	25
Callow, J.	5–60	(6)12–30–35	12, 15–7c

	1966	1967	1968
Callow, W.	12–50	3–30, 140–240	(12)25–340
Cameron, Sir D. Y.	21–25	20–65, 80	6, 90–120
Cameron, Katherine			16
Cameron, Sir P.			75
Campbell, R.	6		
Campion, G. B.	6–15–60	12, 22–35	10, 18–40
Canella, A.		3–9	5–8–16
Canziana, Extella	4–6		30
Cardinal, A.	15		
Carelli, G.		3–20	3
Carmichael, J. W.	(5)35–40	(6)14–40	45–85–120–150
Carpenter, P.			4–40(18)
Carstairs, J. P.			10
Carter, H. B.	4–18	2–14–20	(12)25
Carter, J. N.		18	
Carter, W.		10	30
Casson, Sir H.		7–12	6
Cattermole, C.	8–12	4–15	12–50
Cattermole, G.		2–12	6–40–65
Catton, C.			115
Cayley, N.		50	
Cesar			35
Chadwick, L.	40	50	50–70
Chalon, A. E.	47–50	25–40	10–12, 70
Chalon, H. B.	9–18	15	
Chalon, J. J.		7–10	21–70
Chambers, G.	30	4–20, 45	25–60
Chandra, A.		20–35	

	1966	1967	1968
Chapman, J. W.	5		
Chappell, A.	23		
Charleburg, F.			8
Charlet, N.		18	
Charlton, J.			3
Chase, C.	60	22	6
Chase, G.			6
Chatelaine, J. B.	25		150
Chialiva, L.			12–42
Child, L.		22	6
Chinese School (nineteenth century)	2–4–8	10–18	10
Chinnery, G.	6–22–140	4–20–60	4–27, 110–800
Chipart, L.			50
Chopping, R.			6
Church, C.	5	2–4	18–57
Churchyard, T.	22–35	10–50	4–7, 45–50
Cipriani, G. B.	9–25–80	6–35	(10–18)25–60
Clare, O.	30–100		50
Clare, V.	8–20		
Clarendon, K.			9
Clark, J.			42
Clarke, J. C.			3
Clarke, J. Heaviside Waterloo			60
Clausen, Sir G.	5–15	(4)10–15–24	(4)10–60
Clausen, Katherine			20
Cleaver, R.	1		
Clennell, L.	30		2
Clerihew, W.			20–65–90

7

	1966	*1967*	*1968*
Cook, H. M.		4	12
Cook, S.		25	
Cooke, E. W.	12	12–22–50	16–25–45
Cooper, E.			12
Cooper, R.	10–30		30–100
Cooper, T. S.	2–35	12–25–80	15–35, 100–180
Cope, C. W.	10		5–10
Cope-West, C.			7–12, 40–120
Copley, J. S.			360–780–2300
Corbino, J.	18		
Corbold, R.	4		
Corbould, E. H.			20–31
Cordomer, Rev. C.			115
Cornish, H.	20–28	30–45	
Corrodi, H.			9
Corrodi, S.			45–60
Corvino, J.	18		
Cosway, Maria			35–65
Cosway, R.	25–300	16–40–140	21–25, 380
Cotes, F.	2–12	(12)	12
Cotman, J. J.	60–62	18, 150–160	37–45–180
Cotman, J. S.	10(30)38–230	22–60–300	(25)40–750
Cotman, M. E.	8–60, 100	20–140	10–25, 55–130
Coward, N.			32–42
Cowper, F. C.	2		
Cox, D. (Junior)	7–15	12–33	16–48
Cox, D. (Senior)	(8)15–220	(11)38–120	(12–25)420
Cozens, A.	18–50–189	(12)60	7, 80–1000–3800

	1966	1967	1968
Dalzeil, E. G.	12		
Danby, F.	9–18, 60–100	4–15	25–40–100
Danby, T.	10	16	8–20
Danby, W.		20	30
Devaria, E.		12–18	
Da Costa, L.		25	
Dance, G.	22–45, 200–300	5–45, 200	(6)15–65–168
Dance, N.		15	40–95
D'Andiran, F–F.		20	
Daniel, S.		5	
Danloux			60
Danniell, W.	8–11	30–42	(18)18–60
Darwin, Sir R.		8–30–35	8
David, G.			6–8
David, J.	5	4	
David, Leonie		5	5–10
Davidson, C.		5	
Davidson, T.			5–6
Davies, Warren		5	
Davis, B. A.		8	
Davis, E. T.			25
Davis, J. Scarlett		18	284
Davis, R.			8
Davis, W. H.			18
Dawe, G.			25
Dawson, M.	68–260	95–300	45–150–295
Dawson, N.	2	3	
Day, A.		3	
Day, W.	3–4	15	10–60
Dayes, E.	(18)60–850	18–48, 130–500 1050	20–40–110 400–2700

	1966	1967	1968
De Blaas, E.			10–20
De Breanski		10	4–18
De Chaume			2
D'Egville, J. R.			10
De Francia	8		
De Glehn, W.			18
De Klerk, W.		12	12
De La Bere, S. B.			4
De La Roche, P.			32
De Loutherbourg	40–85, 240	80	23–60, 147–168
De Lynden, Baroness	2–3		
De Martino, E.			47
De Morgan, Evelyn	120		180–200
De Prades, A. F.		5	
De Simone			8
De Sinety		23	
De Wilde, S.		38	18
De Wint, P.	(12)18–140–315	(6–35)55–90–320	(15–20) 40–55
Deane, W. W.		4–10	18
Deangelisse, P. A.			10
Delamotte, W.		6–12	
Des Garets, Oddette		6	
Detaille, E.	12–120		
Detmold, E. J.			8–22
Devis, A.	8–16–18	18–30–57	19–55, 220
Dibdin, T. C.	40–60	50	21–30
Dickee, E. O.		2–4	
Dicksee, Sir, F.	8		

	1966	1967	1968
Dighton, D.		8–28	60–115
Dighton, R.	6–18	5–15, 100	20–25
Dillon, F.			15
Dillon, J.			304
Dixon, C. T.	5–8	6(8)30	7–90
Dobson, F.	10–25	18–35	10–30
Dobson, H. J.	5		
Dobson, W. C. T.	22		15
Dodd, F.	4–12	6–8	4–10
Dodd, J. J.	22	28	
Dodd, R.	28		
Dodgson, G. H.	5–15		22
Dolland, W. A.		4–14	14
Dollman, J. C.			14
Doré, G.		60	10–60, 189–350
D'Orsay, A.		(2)	(10)
Downman, J.	25–60	18–50, 260	(10)55–80
Doyle, R.	7	28	(20)150–1100
D'Oyley, Sir C.	30	25–30	
Drage, J. H.			20
Dring, W.	5		5
Drummond, J.	10		
Drummond-Fish	3		10
Du Creac, J.			12
Du Creux, J.			12
Ducros, P.			32
Duffield, Mary E.			15
Dulac, E.	50	(6)43–92	6–50
Du Maurier	7–11	(2)12–30	5–28
Duncan, E.	4–8, 35, 400	4–6, 38–150	5–45, 85–90

	1966	1967	1968
Epstein, Sir J.	130–250	130–400	120–336
Esposito, D.		15	
Essex, R. H.	20		
Etty, W.	4–25–35	5–80	6–12–35
Evans, B.	15	17–28	2–18
Evans, S.		16	230
Evans, W. (of Eton)	14–50	40–85	18–100–150
Evans, W. (of Bristol)			84
Eves, R. G.	6		
Ewbank, J.			2–5
Eyles, L.	30		
Eyre, E.		95	
Faed, J.			7
Falconet, P.			42–57
Farleigh, J.	15		
Farley, J.			26–29
Farnborough, Lady		20	
Farquharson, J. A.	8		
Farrow, W.		2	
Farrington, J.	6–24–75	(10)50–85	47–90, 150–210
Feary, J.			15
Fedden, R.		4	
Fenn, H.		32	32
Field, N.	5	14–15	
Fielding, A. V. C.	18–160	(2)15–30 35–240	(10)28–90 150–330
Fielding, N.	14	8–15	
Fielding, Thales	14		12
Finart, N. D.		18	

	1966	*1967*	*1968*
Fraser, Lovat	10–15		
Frazer, R. W.	5	4–5	
Freebairn, K.			50
Freeth, H. A.			20–22
French, Annie		75	80–90
French School	10–18–20	2–8–15–25	
Frere, E.	30		
Freud, L.			52–75–120
Friend, D.	10		
Friend, W. F.		42	
Frink, Elizabeth	25		200
Fripp, A. D.			25
Fripp, G. A.	8–25	3–14, 22	16–37, 65
Frith, E.	7–28	28	
Frith, W. P.	15	15	15–28
Frood, Hester			4
Frost, G. (of Ipswich)	3–18	4	(6)15
Frost, W. E.	4–23	5–10–42	10–30–65
Fry, R.			30–38
Fulleylove, J.	4–15, 22–25		20–300
Fullwood, J.			8–50
Furniss, H. J.			18
Fuseli, H.	(22)105	(50)65–1500	(20)55–1500,
Gabriel, Mrs.			6
Gabrini, P.		40	
Gage, Sir T.	40	18–23	
Gainsborough, Sir T.	(12–15) 45–130	(6–10) 18–1000	(20)50–240, 1150–1470
Gale, W.	4		
Gallow, W.		50	

	1966	*1967*	*1968*
Gilpin, S.	16–60		(8)10–46, 70–147
Gilpin, Rev. W.	4–6–20	18–27	4–5(6)
Ginain, E.		26–60	26
Ginner, C.	75		32
Gioja, G.		10	
Girardin, Pauline			18
Girtin, T.	15, 80–150	(6)20–50, 50–300	(10–18) 70–500
Giusti, G.			20–33
Glendenning, A. (Junior)			8–12
Glover, J.	5–16–50	12–15–150	(3–12)32
Goff	4	4–14	
Goodall, E. A. G.	2, 20–28–40	8, 18–22	10–14, 25–40
Goodall, W.		18	
Gooden, J. C.			55–60
Goodwin, A.	12–25	25–40, 120	15–70, 220–260
Gordon, Lady			12
Gore, C.	30		94
Gore, S.	20–40		
Gotch, T. C.	10		
Gould, Sir F.			2–10–90
Grant, C.	3		
Grant, D.	8–15		
Grant, Sir F.	8–12	5–7–18	5
Grant, J.	5		
Gravelot, H. F.	18		
Gray, R.			25
Greaves, H. & W.		30–42	240
Greaves, W.	5–18, 25–75	8–20–30	23–40–170, 420

	1966	*1967*	*1968*
Hale, W.			32
Hall, C.	5–8		
Hall, G. L.			12
Hall, O.		3	25
Halsboom, G.	8		
Halswelle, K.		20	20
Hambridge, J.			5
Hamilton, Lady	22		
Hamilton, H. D.	38	10–18	35
Hamilton, W.	30	(40)5	6–12–25(15)
Hammond, Gertrude, D.		10	
Hammond, K.		5	
Hamnett, Nina			10–22–63
Hancock, F.		2	
Hand, T. H. H.		12	
Hankey, L.		3–6	3–12
Hansen, H.		4	
Hardie, C. M.		10	10–20
Harding, E.			12
Harding, J. D.	5–14–38	(5)6–17	(10)20–100
Harding, S.			33
Hardwick, J. J.		15	18
Hardy, D.	4–6	6–10	3–22–33
Hardy, F.	5		
Hardy, H.		38	
Hardy, J.	6–10, 35–70	7–20	(8)32–42
Hardy, T. B.	(5–12)8–10	9, 25–27	18–50–180
Hare, A.	8		14
Hargitt, E.		25	
Harley, G.	3		

	1966	1967	1968
Harlow, G. H.	2–50	100	28
Harper, J. (of York)			15
Harrington, C.	35	16	32
Harriot, W. W.	3–4	2	
Harrison, G. H.		50	
Harrison, J.			28
Hart, T. G.	2		11–20
Hartmann, J.-J.		170	
Hartnick, A. S.	8		
Harvey, Sir G.		18	
Hassel, E.	12		
Hassel, J.	8	5–10–20	8
Hastings, E.			50
Havell, A. C.	11		
Havell, R.	6		
Havell, W.	4–45	6–40	15–35–110
Hawkesworth, J. H.		5	
Haydon, B. R.	12–15		25–42
Hayes, C.	12		15
Hayes, E.			8
Hayes, W.			80
Hayman, F.	55		126–735
Hayman, P.	5		
Hayter, Sir G.	10–12	6–18	4
Hayter, J.	7–8		(5)4–12, 35
Heaphy, T.	15	12	45
Hearne, T.	70–220	20–32, 110–220	10–30, 65–231,
Heath, W.	20		22
Heathcote, H. M.		10	
Heaton, C.		18	
Helder, C.		20	

	1966	*1967*	*1968*
Hemy, N.			22
Henderson, C. C.	2–20	2–18–25	15, 60–130
Henderson, C. J.			10–25
Henderson, K.		38	
Hendig, H. W.			10
Henshall, H.		12	
Hepworth, Barbara	130–300		
Herald, J.			50
Herbert, A.		35–50	
Herbert, J. R.	15	8–28	6–35–40
Hering, C. E.		8	
Heriot, G.		30	30–150
Herkomer, Sir H. V.	3	4	
Herman, J.	40–65		
Hermann, L.	8	20–25–30	
Hermes, Gertrude		18	
Hern, G. E.		18	
Herring, J. F. (Senior)	29	27–32	(17)28–85
Herring, J. F. (Junior)		38	8
Heysen, H.		30	
Hibbert			(8)
Hicks, L.			20
Highmore, A.			57
Hill, J.		30	
Hill, Rowland		3	50–100
Hills, Robert	5, 40–70	4–11, 25–89	4–15–35
Hine, A. M.			4
Hine, H. G.	8	16–20	25

	1966	1967	1968
Joy, W.	38	36	2, 70–75
Joy, W. & J.	120		
Joyant, J. R.	35		
Julia, Lady Gordon		12–28	24
Jungblut, J.		18	
Jungman, N.			70
Jutsum, H.			60
Kaisermann, F.		75	130
Kalmakoff, H.			50–130
Kauffer, E. M.		5	
Kauffmann, Angelica		(15)15–30	18–105
Kaufy, F. M.		1	
Kearney, J.			190
Kearney, W. H.			60
Keene, C.	12–30	(12)14–40	5–14, 55–200
Keiserman, J. H.	55	85	
Kelly, R. T.	2		10
Kemp-Welch, Lucy	10		6
Kennington, E.	16	15–30	50
Kenrick, G. W.	2		
Kern, M.		8	
Kilburne, G. G.	4–10	6–15	6–12–22
King, B.			6
King, W.			28
King, Y.		8	
Kinnaird, J.			6
Kirby, J.			94
Kitchingham, J.		20	20
Klee, Paul			1100–9000

	1966	1967	1968
Knapton, G.		12	15
Kneale, B.	30		
Kneller, Sir G.	(5)8–110	20–50	70
Knight, J. Baverstock	16–32	3–6	24
Knight, J. Buxton			14
Knight, Dame Laura	55	22–55	10–22–110
Knox, G. J.	5		
Kollmann, R.	34		
Koekkoek, B. C.			50
Koekkoek, J. H.			2
Kramer, J.	12	4–5	
Kretchmer, R.	4–5		
Krieghoff, C.		50	(11)
Krishna, Mary			5
Kyd, J. C. T.			3–5
La Cave, P.	5–10, 25–30		18–25, 45–500
Laby, A.			14
Ladbrooke, J. B.		5–8, 40	
Ladbrooke, R.	80–180		
Laguerre, L.		2	
Laing, F.		5, 90	
Lait, E. B.		3–4	
Lake, P.		6	
Lamb, H. B.		6–7	30
Lambert, J. E.			18–45
Lambourne, N.	6–10	10–15	7–35
Lancaster, O.			6
Lancaster, P.	3	6	6–30
Lance, G.	25		
Landseer, C.		2	1–5

	1966	1967	1968
Landseer Sir, E. H.	8–15, 45–120	6–18, 65–160	18–38–250
Langley, W.			6
Lanyon, P.	20		
Laporte, J.	(5)11–60	(15)40–140	24–45, 140
Laroon, M.			5–23
Lascelles, T.	15		
Last, E. R.	5		5–22
Lavery, Sir J.	22		12
Law, D.	8		
Lawrence, Edith		8	
Lawrence, Sir T.	40–50	336–380–1, 900	40–1100
Lawson, K.	1–2		8
Leader, B. W.			22
Lear, E.	(8)40–80, 160–320	25–40, 90–550	16–35, 320–1500
Le Brocquy, L.		28–30	
Le Capelaine, J.		10	
Ledward, G.	3		
Lee, C.			10
Lee, W.			15
Leech, J.	3–6, 40–45	3–15, 20–60, 78	(7)5–30
Lees, D.	22–35	35	35
Legros, A.	4	6–15	5–18, 30–70–78
Leighton, F. Lord	10–20	11–35–200	10–27, 63–130
Leitch, R. P.	7	5	
Leitch, W. L.	5–14, 20–70	12–30–38	(6)8–32–50
Le Jeune, L. F.		18	
Leman, R.			6–10, 40–150

	1966	1967	1968
Lemeunier, C.			8
Lens, B.			23, 840
Leporte, T. M.		40–70	
Lepsius, R.			32
Leslie, C. R.		178	
Lessore, J.	10		12
Lessore, Thérèse	7–12		12
Léveque, H.	9–11	11	
Levy, M.	7	6	10
Lewin, W.			80–650
Lewis, G. R.	6		
Lewis, J. F.	100	50–150	20–110, 400–5200
Lewis, P. Wyndham	48–70	35–50	160
L'Hermite, L.			32
Liddersdale, C. S.			6
Liddle			12
Lightbody, R.			10
Linaut, T.		7	
Linck, J. A.		1–4	
Lindner, P. M.	5	6	6
Lindner, R.			220
Lindsay, Lady Charlotte	15		
Lindsay, N.	19		
Lindsay, T.	2–30	21	
Linell, C.		4	
Lines, H.		40	
Lines, S.	30		
Linnell, J.		50–65–90	35–900
Linnell, W.			40–60

	1966	1967	1968
Linton, Sir J.	5	6	
Linton, W.			7–20
Linwood, Mary			95
Lister, Harriet		10	
Livens, H. M.		8	5–10–20
Lloyd, J.			200
Lloyd, R. M.			16, 147–210
Locatelli, A.			11
Lock, C.		70	
Lock, W.		70	
Lockhart, W. E.			14
Lodge, G. E.	(1)30–57		35–45
Lodge, R. B.		4	
Lodge, T.	8		
Lomax, R. L.		15	15
Longshift, W.	18		
Lory, G. L.			75
Loubon, E.		10	
Louisa, Marchioness of Waterford	14–18		15–20
Lound, T.	10–20	28–50	12, 42–120
Lover, S.		6	
Low, R.		12	
Lowry, L. S.	250		28, 150–300
Luard, L.			14–18
Lucas, E.			120
Lucas, J. S.	9		4
Lundgen, E.			8–15–32–160
Lutyens, Sir, E.			95
Lyne, M.			15–32
Maccoll, D. S.	2	2	6–30

	1966	*1967*	*1968*
Martineau, Edith	15–22		
Martineau, G. M.			18
Mason, F.			6
Master of the Giants	84		
Matania, F.		40–70	
Mattino, I.	5		
Mauton, Signor		19	
Mauve, A.	50	55	10–15
May, W. W. ('Phil')	6–15	3–10	5–11, 35
Mayor, B.			90
Maze, P.	45–70	25–80	15, 80–160
McBey, J.		35	4–50
McEvoy, A.	12–20–40, 380		7–28–80
McMorland, P. J.			13
McWhirter, Agnes Eliza			50
Meadows, J. E.		16–23	
Meissonier, J. L. E.	50		12–170
Melbye, A.			10–45
Melville, A.			65–80
Melville, H. S.	20		
Mends, T. C.			7
Meneghini, M.			27
Meninsky, B.	3–10–20	14	35–55
Menpes, M.		4–25	
Mercey, F.			3
Merritt, N. R.			2
Meteyard, Lady H.		18	18

	1966	1967	1968
Methuen, Lord			14–38
Meyer, A. J.	4–5	4–35	
Middleditch, E.	40		
Middleton, E.	160	120	100
Middleton, C.		16	
Migliaro, V.		38	
Mildmay, C. S.			10
Millais, Sir J. E.	(8)35–38, 136–178	(18)380–2100	30–45, 60–950
Millais, J. G.		4–5	4–5–20
Millais, R.	7		16–28
Millais, W. H.		30–40–170	15, 90–170, 336
Miller, J.		30	
Miller, W.	45	10	
Millington, J. (Junior)		30	10
Milne, J. M.	18–120		
Milner, W.	2		68
Minorcan School (nineteenth century)		28	
Minton, J.	15	20–25–30–42	42–60, 130–190
Mitchell, P.			7
Mogford, J.	7–8	16–40	15–25
Moira, G.	18		
Mole, J. H.	7–20, 35	8–12, 30	8, 25–40
Monamy, P.			60
Monk, W.		3	
Monro, J.		6	
Monro, Dr. T.	6–12	(2)8–18	6–8–30
Montanaro, A.			57

	1966	*1967*	*1968*
Moore, A.			550
Moore, H.	8		
Moore, Henry	2, 500, 120–500		650, 1050–1100
Moore, J.			90
Moore, W. (of York)	6–10		
Mordaunt, Lady	5		10
Morland, G.	(20)6–25	10–40, 75–90	23–50, 90–300
Morphew, R.			30
Morris, Max			2
Morris, O.		25	
Morris, W.		140–210	
Morrow, G.	3		
Mortimer, J. H.	22–18	25–45	20–55, 60–297
Moser, G. M.	18		(5)840
Muckley, W. J.			60
Muirhead, D.			14–16
Muirhead, W. J.			14
Mulholland, J.	18		
Muller, P. A.			18
Muller, R. A.			22
Muller, W. J.	25–47	10, 95	(8)18–38, 75–300
Mulready, A. E.		68	20–30
Mulready, W.	25	40	2, 20–50
Muncaster, C.	5–6	2–12	6–10
Munn, P. S.	7–28	16–45	8–25–80
Munnings, Sir A.	25–70–80–140	12–32, 130	20–50, 130–1200

	1966	*1967*	*1968*
New, E. L.			40
New Zealand School			15
Newhouse, C. B.		80	50
Newman, H.			42
Newton, A. P.	5		136
Newton, R.	44		
Nibbs, R. H.	2–5	6, 25–30	5–10
Nichol, A.	18	3–30–45	(8)65–90
Nichols, B.			12
Nichols, J.			4
Nicholson, B.	550		550
Nicholson, F.	7–18, 75–165	6–12, 50–80	(15)20–70–170
Nicholson, G. S.	2	10	3
Nicholson, J.			12
Nicholson, Sir W.			48–120
Nicholson, Winifred	130		
Nicol, E.	3–20	2–5, 20–35	2–12–26
Nicolet, G. E. E.			6
Nicolson, T. H.			4
Niedham, J.	3–18		
Nielson, K.			150–273
Nieman, E. J.	18	15	7–38
Ninham, H.		5–7	
Nixon, A. J.	170		15, 105–470
Nixon, S.	(15)170		(4)
Noirot, E.		15	
Nolan, S.		15–18	
Nollekens, J.			5–20
Norie, F.	2		4
Norie, O.		17–28	38–40–57

	1966	1967	1968
Normand, A.			18
Norrington		26	
North, J. W.	10–40	5	
Norwich School			25
Nurfe, W.			75
Nutter, W. H.	22		21
Oakes, J. W.			10
Oakley, O. 'Gipsy'			8–22–58
O'Brien	8		
Ogle, J. C.		40	
Oldfield, J. E.	20	10	30
Oliver, Emma	5		10
Oliver, W.	15–30	6–30	35
O'Meara, F.	15		
O'Neill, G. B.	8		
O'Niell, N.	7		
Ongania, U.		6–12–25	5–6–15
Opie, J.			38
Oran, W.	60		
Ormond, L.			3–4
Orpen, Sir W.	10–17–40	20–25	20–55–75
Orrock, J.	5–15–32	6–17–25	10–20
Ottley, W. Y.	10		
Ouvrié, J.		35–38–42	
Owen, S.	6, 20–75	22–35	12–18, 25–130
Owen, W.			15
Page, M. A.	35		
Page, R. M.	50		
Paget-Lucens, Capt.			8
Palmer, G.			10

9+

	1966	1967	1968
Powell, T.		8	
Poynter, Sir E. J.	5–18	11–20	12–15, 30–105
Prentice, J. P.	5		25
Priest, A.		45	25–550
Priestman, B.	10		
Printz		6	
Prior, M.			10
Prior, W. H.	5		
Pritchett, E.	50–200	(8)20–40	
Procktor, P.	35–40		
Prosser, H.			15
Prout, Samuel	(6)9–25, 85	8–15, 35–48–60	(6)15–20, 60–160
Prout, Skinner J.	8	6–8, 35–60	6–12–45
Pryde, J.			35
Pugin, A. W. N.		35	35
Pugh, H.			21
Purser, W.			65
Puzzuli			4
Pye, W.		10	
Pyne, G. B.	12–18, 35–190	25–100	18–85–250
Pyne, James Baker	16–190	15–40	140–300
Pyne, T.	5	6	
Pyne, W. H.		10–15	30–48
Rabin, S.		6	
Rackham, A.	20–30		30, 170–250
Rackham, Edith S.			60–63
Radcliffe, C. W.	5		35–65
Raeburn			(10)
Rainey, W.	2		
Ramsay, A.	20–30	28	(2)18–28

	1966	1967	1968
Richardson, T. M. (Senior)	28–45	15–36	4, 25–57
Richardson, T. M. (Junior)	15–29	20–35–58	16–45–100
Richmond, B.			5
Richmond, G.	6–20	20–25, 840	8
Richmond, Laura	2		
Richmond, Sir W. B.	4–6		9
Richter, H. D.			10
Ricketts, C.	55–130		
Rickman, P.	25	5–16	20–22
Riddell, R. A.	25–120		
Rider, F.	2		
Riepl, Aloisia		5	
Rigby, C.	5		
Riley, J.	5	20–50	
Rimble, E.		8	
Ritchie, A. P.	4		
Riviere, B.	8–14–42		42
Riviere, H. J.	5	28	
Roberti, R. M.		20	
Roberts, D.	10–45, 130–270	20–55, 140–380	(5–22) 20–100, 320–440, 440–1680
Roberts, H. B.	15		140–440
Roberts, P.			30
Roberts, T. J.			63
Roberts, W.	12–16	15	20–30
Robertson, J.	4–10	12	
Robertson, W. G.	55		20

9*

	1966	1967	1968
Roussoff, A. N.			29
Rowbotham, C.	6–15	10–12–18–22	12–26
Rowbotham, T. L. (Senior)	10–12	6–45–55	22–25–28
Rowbotham, T. L. (Junior)	18–20	10–12–22	40
Rowe, G.	16		
Rowlandson, T.	16–30 280–300, 1500	18–45–50 700–1500, 11000	(7–18)60–90 190–11000
Rowntree, H.			4
Rudge, L.			12
Runciman, A.			230
Rushbury, Sir H.		15	16–22
Rushbury, T. H.	5–8	25	16–30
Ruskin, J.	40–50, 95–120	6–15, 90–540, 900	20–55
Russell, J.	17–25	4–18, 40–250	40–55, 157–315
Russell, Sir W.			48
Rutherston, A. D.	15–30	35	25–80
Ryland, H.		8	12–90
Rysbrack, J. M.			147
Saint-Cyr, H. G.			20–40
St. John, E.		2	16
Salmon, J. C.		22	7–23
Salsbury, F. O.	50		
Samuel, G.	35–40		
Sandby, P.	(3–12)60–70, 1500	(10–16)40–80, 367	(20)33–100, 200–750, 1250–6000
Sandby, T.	45		31
Sander, T.	50		

	1966	*1967*	*1968*
Senior, W.			4
Serres, D. M.	28–80	44	(22)55–80, 115–340
Serres, J. T.	(10)18–28	(20)200–300	(6)35–75
Settle, W. E.			13
Settle, W. H. S.			28
Severn, A.		40	40–50
Severn, J. A. P.			2–10, 110
Severn, W.			12
Seymour, J.		28	(15)10–28–50
Shackleton, W.	8		15
Shalders, G.	12		
Shannon, C.	7–20	8–25	2–12–50
Sharp, C. K.			17
Sharples, J.			55
Shaw, J. B.			4–55
Shayer, W.		150	
Shee, Sir, M. A.			200
Sheffield, G.			19
Shelley, S.		28	5–15
Shepard, E. H.	8		20
Shepheard, G. W.		26	
Shepherd, G.		18–26	6–32
Shepherd, G. S.	3–8, 45–100	12–32–70	18, 100–200
Shepherd, R.		8	
Shepherd, T. H.	20–42	16–48	15–48–70
Sheridan, K. G.	5		
Sheringham, G.		3–17	
Sherman, W.		200	10
Sherrin, J.	16		22
Shields, F.		15	

	1966	1967	1968
Smith, J. Clarendon			35
Smith, J. Burrell		4	10–30
Smith, J. Raphael	18–20	5–800	28–60, 800–900
Smith, J. 'Warwick'	40–100	(16)20–35, 620	12–32–80–200
Smith, Sir M.	90–220		115
Smith, S.	130		
Smith of Chichester		6	
Smyth, L.		10	
Smyth, S. R.		30	
Smyth, W.		30	
Smythe, Minnie	5		
Smythe, T.	4–65		65
Solomon, A.	9		
Solomon, E.			10
Solomon, S.	8–18–27	20–60	10–12, 65–90
South American School			100
Southgate, F.		22	2
Souza, F.		6	18
Spackman, C. S.	2		11
Spackman, I.	8		80
Spalding, C. B.			15
Spanish School			25
Spare, A. O.	12	2–14	6–12–32–40
Speechley, W.			120
Speed, H.			10
Spencelagh, C.	110	2–5–14	
Spencer, Caroline			22

	1966	*1967*	*1968*
Spencer, G.	20–38	12	
Spencer, Sir S.	55–80	10–22	35–48–90
Spencer, T. R.	5		
Spenlove, S. F.	3		
Spurling, J.			80
'Spy'			10
Squirrel, L. R.	3–15	10	
Staines, W. T.	6		6
Stanfield, G. Clarkson	(5–30), 10–100	(12)5, 10–48	(8)32–40, 120–360
Stanley, C. R.			16
Stannard, Eloise			6–35, 170
Stannard, H. S.	6		5
Stannard, J.	30		20
Stannard, Lilian		3	
Stanwyck, H.			8
Stark, A.	8		
Stark, J.	(8)20–35, 65–168	20–45–90	25–70–160
Starr, Louise	2		
Staveley, W.		30–40–60	
Steele, Louise	5		
Steelink, W.		6	
Steeple, J.		5	
Steer, P. Wilson	14–60–105	(20)25–60, 90	16–20, 140–270
Stephanoff, F. P.	4		38–50–73
Stevens, A.		5–18	10–20–40
Stewart, F. A.		48–78	
Stewart, Sir J.	6–15	12	12
Stillman, Marie		68	
Stock, H. J.		6–18	38

	1966	1967	1968
Stocks, B.			40
Stockdale, F.		15	
Stockdale, W. L.		7	
Stokes, A.		5	
Stone, F.	12		
Stone, M.			20
Stone, R.	20		
Stone, Sarah		18–75	18
Stothard, T.	8		16–24–50–84–115
Stott, E.			32
Strang, W.	5–8	8–12	15–18, 90
Strutt, E. J.	10		
Stuart, Sir J. J.	9–18	8–26	12
Stuart, J. 'Athenian'			300
Stubbs, G.			1150
Suddaby, R.			15–16
Sullivan, J. F.		1	
Sully, T.	45	40	
Summarie, G.		8	
Sunderland, T.	4–16	5–38–20	12–15–50
Sutherland, G.	300–650		262–300–1200
Swaine, F.	25		9, 150–190
Swan, J. M.	25	20–22	22–30
Swete, Rev. J.	2–4		5–20
Swinburne, E.			60
Swinburne, Julie	20		
Swiss School	8–10	12–18	7–10
Syer, J.	5		10–12
Sykes, C.	3		
Talbot-Kelly, R.			9

	1966	1967	1968
Tromp, J. Z.		8	
Trotman, Lillie			6
Trouillebert, P. D.		6	
Tryon, W.			8
Tucker, A.		3	
Tucker, E.			5–10
Tudor, T.	26		1–25
Tuke, H. S.	32	8–25, 40–60	16–28, 50–170
Tunnard, J.	120		60–90–120
Tunnicliffe, C. F.			28–60
Turkish School			4
Turnbull, W.	15	40	
Turner, J.			25
Turner, J. M. W.	(10–25) 18–330	(18–105) 240–400, 3000–5200	(14–75) 110–150, 520–900
Turner, R.		36	15
Turner, W. (of Oxford)	6–40	15–30, 70–90	10–70, 170–470,
Turpin, P. J. F.			75
Tyndale, W.			15
Underhill, F. C.			15
Underwood, L.			22
Unterberger			(25)
Unwin			(18)
Upton, M.	10		
Utterson, E. V.	20–35	12–20–60	28–60
Utterson, Louisa	30		
Uwins, T.	18	45–130	10–45, 130
Vacher, C.	12	2	6
Valentino, A.			25
Van de Velde (the Younger)	21–25	20–24	20–90

	1966	*1967*	*1968*
Wain, L.	3–10	2–3, 38	4–15–20
Wainwright, W.	7		
Waite, R. T.	6		
Wakeman, T.		18	
Walcot, W.	20		
Wale, S.	5–25		15–20, 78–336
Walker, A.			157
Walker, Dame Ethel			18–22
Walker, F.	2–15–30	7–10	10–25
Walker, W. H.	3		7
Wall, W. L.	30		
Wall-Callcott, Sir J.	10–25	10	
Wallace, Florence			4
Wallace, R.	4	4	
Waller, H.		5	12
Wallis, A.	65–85		25–38, 100–220
Wallis, J.	25		
Walmsley, T.			20
Walsh, T.			10
Walters, G. S.	4–5	4	4–8, 16–20
Walton, E.	3–10, 25–40		25–38
Walton, F.			36
Ward, C.			1–12
Ward, E. M.		25	
Ward, James	15–25, 55–300	(18)28–35	(25)110–280– 480
Ward, John	22		25–78
Ward, W.	1		85, 370–950
Warington, T.			3

	1966	1967	1968
Warren, E. G.	8		
Warren, H.	18		
Warrener, W. T.		32	
Warwick, George Earl of			1–2
Waterford, Lady		12	
Waterhouse, A.	6		12
Waterhouse, J. W.			68
Waterlow, Sir E. A.	5		12
Watson, H.	5		6
Watson, Jane	28		95
Watson, J. D.		3	
Watts, F. W.	65	10	
Watts, G. F.	20		
Way, T. R.			15
Weatherall, H.	10		12
Weatherill, G.	5–10		11–22
Weaver, M.		2	
Webb, J. E.	5	4	30
Webster, T.		120	
Weedon, A. W.		35	
Wehnert, E. H.		25	10
Weicall, C. H.			12
Weight, C.	20–30		
Weir, H.		10	
Welch, D.		15–22	6–18–52
Welch, Lucy Kemp	10		6
Wells, J. S.			14–60
Wells, W. F.	3–20	3–15	55–147
Wepel, J.		16	

	1966	1967	1968
Werner, C.	28	3–20	
Werner, K. F.			22
West, B.	6–16–32–100	18–60, 250–350	(25)32–40, 57–350
West, E. E.		6–20, 130–420	
West, J. W.	5–10	15	4–16
West, R. L.	10	10–12	45–50
West, W. 'Norwegian'		4	
Westall, R.	3–18	10–30	(4)18–65
Westall, W.		10–27	65
Whatley, H.	35		
Wheatley, F.	15–35, 120	(5)40–160, 350–800	(10–42) 168–470– 900
Whichelo, J.			30
Whistler, J. A. M.	157, 348–450	(35)	30–35, 150–320
Whistler, Mrs. M.		12	
Whistler, R.		40–55–320	30–95–110
White, E.	14		20–25–42
White, G. F.			32
Whitely, B.	18		
Whiting, A.			25
Widala		4	
Widgery, W.		4–5	2–4
Wilcox, J.			4
Wild, C.	40	12	31
Wille, P. A.		30	
Wilkie, Sir D.	10–30, 40–75	8–18, 29–50	8–18, 40–180
Wilkinson, Rev. J.	4–10	8–12	13
Wilkinson, N.	7		15

	1966	*1967*	*1968*
Williams, H. 'Grecian'	5	10–25	14, 30–120–150
Williams, P.	30	5	
Williams, R.	6		5
Williamson, F.			5
Wilson, C.			18
Wilson, C. E.		15–16	
Wilson, H.			20
Wilson, Jock	3–5	5	
Wilson, Richard	20–50, 120	(14)25–205	78–367
Wilson, Scottie		8–30–35	8–12, 25–35
Wilton, J.			50
Wimperis, E. M.	10–20	6–15–20	12–25–45–75
Wingfield, H.	9–45		
Winkworth, W. W.			5
Winship, J.		7	
Winter, G.	4		
Winter, H. T.	5	4–5–6	7
Winter, R.	8		
Winter, T.			5–6
Winterhalter, T. X.			35–50
Winton, J. B.			50
Wintour, J. C.	5		
Withered, V.		4	
Witherington, W. F.			336
Withers, Mrs. Augusta		25	28–80
Wolf, J.		14–42	36
Wolfe, G.			7

	1966	*1967*	*1968*
Wollaston, C. B.	30		
Wolstenholme, D. (Junior)			7
Wood, C.	45–50	35	35–50–100–375
Wood, Eleanour S.		20	
Wood, J.			8–35
Wood, L. S.			3
Wood, T. G.	40		
Woodman, C. H.			22
Woodville, R. C.		1	
Woodward, J. M.	15–28	12–48	(10)28–70
Woodward, W. H.	14		
Woolnoth, C. N.			15
Worlidge, T.	15	90	3, 15–52–126
Wormald, P.			5
Worth, L.	15–20		20
Worthington, T. G.			5
Wren, J. C.			20–29, 200
Wright, Joseph (of Derby)			29–200
Wright, J. Masey	7–18	10–18	8–50
Wright, R. H.			9–22–60
Wright, J. W.			20
Wright, T. (of Derby)	20	10–32	(6)10
Wright, T. (of Newark)	5–12		
Wyeth, P.			35
Wyld, W.		12	5, 65–100

Bibliography

English Watercolours. Laurence Binyon. Black, 1962

An Introduction to English Painting. John Rothenstein. Cassell, 1965

Early English Watercolours. Iolo M. Williams. Connoisseur, 1953

The Art Game. Robert Wraight. Frewin, 1965

British Watercolours. Graham Reynolds. Victoria & Albert Museum, London, H.M.S.O., 1968

Watercolour: Materials and Techniques. George Dibble. Holt, Rinehart and Winston, Inc., New York, 1966

Drawing. Daniel M. Mendelowitz. Holt, Rinehart & Winston, Inc., New York, 1967

British Portrait Miniatures. Daphne Foskett. Methuen, 1963

Water-Colour Painting in Britain. Martin Hardie. Vols. 1, 2, 3. Batsford, 1967–69

Water-Colours of the Norwich School. Derek Clifford. Cory Adams & Mackay, 1965

English Neo-classic Art. David Irwin. Faber, 1966

INDEX

(Numbers in italics refer to illustrations)